This anthology of Chinese poems was compiled and translated by Arthur Waley C.B.E., F.B.S., the distinguished authority on Chinese language and literature. A translator of genius, he received the Queen's medal for poetry in 1953. His many books include *The Tale of Genji, The Way and Its Power* and *Monkey*. He died in 1966.

The poems represented in this collection were chosen for their ability to work in a literal as well as a literary translation. Poems of a highly allusive nature are excluded and annotation is, therefore, kept to a minimum. It is essentially a book of poetry.

CHINESE POEMS

Chinese Poems

ARTHUR WALEY

London
UNWIN PAPERBACKS
Boston   Sydney

First published by George Allen & Unwin 1946
Reprinted four times
First published in paperback 1961
First published in Unwin Paperbacks 1982
This book is copyright under the Berne Convention. No reproduction
without permission. All rights reserved.

UNWIN® PAPERBACKS
40 Museum Street, London WC1A 1LU, UK

Unwin Paperbacks
Park Lane, Hemel Hempstead, Herts HP2 4TE, UK

George Allen & Unwin Australia Pty Ltd,
8 Napier Street, North Sydney, NSW 2060, Australia

© George Allen & Unwin (Publishers) Ltd, 1946, 1961, 1983

ISBN 0 04 895027 0

Set in 9 point Plantin
and printed in Great Britain
by Hazell Watson and Viney Ltd, Aylesbury, Bucks

To
Edith Sitwell

PREFACE TO THE FIRST EDITION

This book contains a selection of poems from *The Book of Songs* (1937) and most of the poems from *170 Chinese Poems* (1918), *More Translations* (1919) and *The Temple* (1923). The poems have been arranged as far as possible in chronological order. All the translations have been thoroughly revised.

The present order of the poems has of course no reference to the dates at which they were translated, and as my methods have changed a good deal in the last thirty years, the reader will find very literal, almost pidgin-English versions side by side with more finished work. I have made very few merely stylistic alterations; but the *Hymn to the Fallen* struck me as definitely bad, and I have, I think, greatly improved it.

Out of the Chinese five-word line I developed between 1916 and 1923 a metre, based on what Gerard Manley Hopkins called 'sprung rhythm', which I believe to be just as much an English metre as blank verse. The Chinese seven-word line is much more difficult to handle and I have not attempted any long poems in this metre.

This brings me to the question of selection. My book is not a balanced anthology of Chinese poetry, but merely a collection of poems that happen to work out well in a literal but at the same time literary translation. This of course excludes poems of a highly allusive nature, requiring an undue amount of annotation. The fact that I have translated ten times more poems by Po Chu-i than by any other writer does not mean that I think him ten times as good as any of the rest, but merely that I find him by far the most remarkable of the major Chinese poets. Nor does it mean that I am unfamiliar with the works of other great T'ang and Sung poets. I have indeed made many attempts to translate Li Po, Tu Fu and Su Shih; but the results have not satisfied me.

This book is intended to be essentially a book of poetry, and I have excluded the biographical and historical essays that formed part, for example, of *170 Chinese Poems*.

1946

PREFACE TO THE FIRST PAPERBACK EDITION

This is a reprint of *Chinese Poems* (1946), except that the Additional Notes have been omitted, and a few translations made since 1946 have been included – a series of poems by Han-shan and a love poem by Fêng Mêng-lung. The Hanshan poems originally appeared in *Encounter* and the love-poem in the *Evergreen Review*. My book is not a balanced and representative anthology of Chinese poetry through the ages, but merely a collection of poems that I like particularly and that happen to work out well in translation. The translations were made over a long period – between 1916 and 1959. I have corrected some mistakes in those made long ago, but in two or three cases I have not altered inaccuracies because I found that I could not do so without spoiling the general effect of the poem. For example on page 53, line 18, lush verdure rather than wetness is implied, but I find it hard to express this satisfactorily.

1960

CONTENTS

FROM THE BOOK OF SONGS

ORIGIN-LEGEND OF THE CHOU TRIBE
(c. 900 B.C.)

SHE who in the beginning gave birth to the people,
This was Chiang Yüan.
How did she give birth to the people?
She sacrificed and prayed
That she might no longer be childless.
She trod on the big toe of God's footprint,
Was accepted and got what she desired.
Then in reverence, then in awe
She gave birth, she nurtured;
And this was Hou Chi.[1]

The mother had fulfilled her months,
And her first-born came like a lamb
With no bursting or rending,
With no hurt or harm.
To make manifest His magic power
God on high gave her ease.
So blessed were her sacrifice and prayer
That easily she bore her child.

They put it in a narrow lane;
But oxen and sheep tenderly cherished it.
They[2] put it in a far-off wood;
But it chanced that woodcutters came to this wood.
They put it on the cold ice;
But the birds covered it with their wings.
The birds at last went away,
And Hou Chi began to wail.

Truly far and wide
His voice was very loud.

[1] 'Lord Millet.'
[2] The ballad does not tell us who exposed the child. According to one
version it was the mother herself; according to another, the husband.

15

Then sure enough he began to crawl;
Well he straddled, well he reared,
To reach food for his mouth.
He planted large beans;
His beans grew fat and tall.
His paddy-lines were close set,
His hemp and wheat grew thick,
His young gourds teemed.

Truly Hou Chi's husbandry
Followed the way that had been shown.[1]
He cleared away the thick grass,
He planted the yellow crop.
It failed nowhere, it grew thick,
It was heavy, it was tall,
It sprouted, it eared,
It was firm and good,
It nodded, it hung—
He made house and home in T'ai.[2]

The lucky grains were sent down to us,
The black millet, the double-kernelled,
Millet pink-sprouted and white.
Far and wide the black and the double-kernelled
He reaped and acred;[3]
Far and wide the millet pink and white
He carried in his arms, he bore on his back,
Brought them home, and created the sacrifice.

What are they, our sacrifices?
We pound the grain, we bale it out,
We sift, we tread,
We wash it—soak, soak;
We boil it all steamy.
Then with due care, due thought
We gather southernwood, make offering of fat,
Take lambs for the rite of expiation,
We roast, we broil,
To give a start to the coming year.

[1] By God.
[2] South-west of Wu-kung Hsien, west of Sianfu. Said to be where his mother came from.
[3] The yield was reckoned per acre (100 ft. square).

High we load the stands,
The stands of wood and of earthenware.
As soon as the smell rises
God on high is very pleased:
'What smell is this, so strong and good?'
Hou-Chi founded the sacrifices,
And without blemish or flaw
They have gone on till now.

SONGS OF COURTSHIP

(Seventh Century B.C. ?)

(1)

OUT in the bushlands a creeper grows,
The falling dew lies thick upon it.
There was a man so lovely,
Clear brow well rounded.
By chance I came across him,
And he let me have my will.

Out in the bushlands a creeper grows,
The falling dew lies heavy on it.
There was a man so lovely,
Well rounded his clear brow.
By chance I came upon him:
'Oh, Sir, to be with you is good.'

(2)

IN the lowlands is the goat's-peach;[1]
Very delicate are its boughs.
Oh, soft and tender,
Glad I am that you have no friend.

In the lowlands is the goat's-peach;
Very delicate are its flowers.
Oh, soft and tender,
Glad I am that you have no home.

[1] The goat's-peach was later identified with the Chinese gooseberry, which now only grows a long way south of the Yangtze. The same names were applied to the *Actinidia Chinensis*, which grows in the north and is probably what is meant here.

17

In the lowlands is the goat's-peach;
Very delicate is its fruit.
Oh, soft and tender,
Glad I am that you have no house.

(3)

PLOP fall the plums; but there are still seven.[1]
Let those gentlemen that would court me
Come while it is lucky!

Plop fall the plums; there are still three.
Let any gentleman that would court me
Come before it is too late!

Plop fall the plums; in shallow baskets we lay them.
Any gentleman who would court me
Had better speak while there is time.

(4)

A VERY handsome gentleman
Waited for me in the lane;
I am sorry I did not go with him.

A very splendid gentleman
Waited for me in the hall;
I am sorry I did not keep company with him.

I am wearing my unlined coat, my coat all of brocade.
I am wearing my unlined skirt, my skirt all of brocade!
Oh, sir, Oh my lord,
Take me with you in your coach!

I am wearing my unlined skirt, my skirt all of brocade.
And my unlined coat, my coat all of brocade.
Oh, sir, oh my lord,
Take me with you in your coach!

---

[1] This poem is akin to love-divinations of the type 'Loves me, loves me not' and 'This year, next year, some time, never.' Seven, as with us, is a lucky number.

OF fair girls the loveliest
Was to meet me at the corner of the Wall.
But she hides and will not show herself;
I scratch my head, pace up and down.

Of fair girls the prettiest
Gave me a red flute.
The flush of that red flute
Is pleasure at the girl's beauty.

She has been in the pastures and brought for me
     rush-wool,
Very beautiful and rare.
It is not you that are beautiful;
But you were given by a lovely girl.

I AM going to gather the dodder
To the south of Mei.[1]
Of whom do I think?
Of lovely Mêng Chiang.
She was to wait for me at Sang-chung,
But she went all the way to Shang-kung
And came with me to the banks of the Ch'i.

I am going to gather goosefoot
To the north of Mei.
Of whom do I think?
Of lovely Mêng I.
She was to wait for me at Sang-chung,
But she went all the way to Shang-kung
And came with me to the banks of the Ch'i.

I am going to gather charlock
To the east of Mei.
Of whom do I think?
Of lovely Mêng Yung.
She was to wait for me at Sang-chung,
But she went all the way to Shang-kung
And came with me to the banks of the Ch'i.

[1] The places mentioned in the song were all in northern Honan.

(7)

I BEG of you, Chung Tzu,
Do not climb into our homestead,
Do not break the willows we have planted.
Not that I mind about the willows,
But I am afraid of my father and mother.
Chung Tzu I dearly love;
But of what my father and mother say
Indeed I am afraid.

I beg of you, Chung Tzu,
Do not climb over our wall,
Do not break the mulberry-trees we have planted.
Not that I mind about the mulberry-trees,
But I am afraid of my brothers.
Chung Tzu I dearly love;
But of what my brothers say
Indeed I am afraid.

I beg of you, Chung Tzu,
Do not climb into our garden,
Do not break the hard-wood we have planted.
Not that I mind about the hard-wood,
But I am afraid of what people will say.
Chung Tzu I dearly love;
But of all that people will say
Indeed I am afraid.

(8)

'THE cock has crowed;
The Court by now is full.'
'It was not the cock that crowed;
It was the buzzing of those green flies.'
'Eastward the sky is bright;
The Court must be in full swing.'
'It is not the light of dawn;
It is the moon that is going to rise.
The gnats fly drowsily;
It will be sweet to share a dream with you.'
Soon all the Courtiers will go home;
Why get us both into this scrape?

20

(9)

Shu is away in the hunting-fields,
There is no one living in our lane.
Of course there *are* people living in our lane;
But they are not like Shu,
So beautiful, so good.

Shu has gone after game,
No one drinks wine in our lane.
Of course people *do* drink wine in our lane;
But they are not like Shu,
So beautiful, so loved.

Shu has gone to the wilds,
No one drives horses in our lane.
Of course people *do* drive horses in our lane.
But they are not like Shu,
So beautiful, so brave.

(10)

Shu in the hunting-fields
Driving his team of four,
The reins like ribbons in his hand,
His helpers[1] leaping as in the dance!
Shu in the prairie.[2]
The flames rise crackling on every side;
Bare-armed he braves a tiger
To lay at the Duke's feet.
Please, Shu, no rashness!
Take care, or it will hurt you.

Shu in the hunting-fields
Driving his team of bays.
The yoke-horses, how high they prance!
Yet the helpers keep line
Like wild-geese winging in the sky.
Shu in the prairie.
Flames leap crackling on every side.
How well he shoots, how cleverly he drives!

[1] The two outside horses.
[2] That has been fired to drive the game into the open.

21

Now giving rein, now pulling to a halt,
Now letting fly,
Now following up his prey.

Shu in the hunting-fields,
Driving a team of greys.
The two yoke-horses with heads in line,
The two helpers obedient to his hand.
Shu in the prairie,
Huge fires crackling on every side.
His horses slow down,
Shu shoots less often.
Now he lays aside his quiver,
Now he puts his bow in its case.

(11)

A MOON rising white
Is the beauty of my lovely one.
Ah, the tenderness, the grace!
Trouble consumes me.

A moon rising bright
Is the fairness of my lovely one.
Ah, the gentle softness!
Trouble torments me.

A moon rising in splendour
Is the beauty of my lovely one.
Ah, the delicate yielding!
Trouble confounds me.

(12)

OUTSIDE the Eastern Gate
Are girls many as the clouds;
But though they are many as clouds
There is none on whom my heart dwells.
White jacket and grey scarf
Alone could cure my woe.

Beyond the Gate Tower
Are girls lovely as rush-wool;
But though they are lovely as rush-wool
There is none with whom my heart bides.
White jacket and madder skirt
Alone could bring me joy.

(13)

Look at that little bay of the Ch'i,
Its kitesfoot so delicately waving.
Delicately fashioned is my lord,
As thing cut, as thing filed,
As thing chiselled, as thing polished.
Oh, the grace, the elegance!
Oh, the lustre, oh, the light!
Delicately fashioned is my lord;
Never for a moment can I forget him.

Look at that little bay of the Ch'i,
Its kitesfoot so fresh.
Delicately fashioned is my lord,
His ear-plugs are of precious stones,
His cap-gems stand out like stars.
Oh, the grace, the elegance!
Oh, the lustre, the light!
Delicately fashioned is my lord;
Never for a moment can I forget him.

Look at that little bay of the Ch'i,
Its kitesfoot in their crowds.
Delicately fashioned is my lord,
As a thing of bronze, a thing of white metal,
As a sceptre of jade, a disc of jade.
How free, how easy
He leant over his chariot-rail!
How cleverly he chaffed and joked,
And yet was never rude!

(14)

If along the highroad
I caught hold of your sleeve,

23

Do not hate me;
Old ways take time to overcome.
If along the highroad
I caught hold of your hand,
Do not be angry with me;
Friendship takes time to overcome.

(15)

By the willows of the Eastern Gate,
Whose leaves are so thick,
At dusk we were to meet;
And now the morning star is bright.

By the willows of the Eastern Gate,
Whose leaves are so close,
At dusk we were to meet;
And now the morning star is pale.

(16)

'I BROUGHT my great carriage that thunders
And a coat downy as rush-wool.
It was not that I did not love you,
But I feared that you had lost heart.

I brought my great carriage that rumbles
And a coat downy as the pink sprouts.[1]
It was not that I did not love you,
But I feared that you would not elope.'

Alive, they never shared a house,
But in death they had the same grave.
'You thought I had broken faith;
I was true as the bright sun above.'

WEDDING SONG

My lord is all a-glow.
In his left hand he holds the reed-pipe,
With his right he summons me to make free with him.
Oh, the joy!

[1] Of red millet.

24

My lord is care-free.
In his left hand he holds the dancing plumes,
With his right he summons me to sport with him.
Oh, the joy!

WIDOW'S LAMENT

THE cloth-plant grew till it covered the thorn bush;
The bindweed spread over the wilds.
My lovely one is here no more.
With whom? No, I sit alone.

The cloth-plant grew till it covered the brambles;
The bindweed spread across the borders of the field.
My lovely one is here no more.
With whom? No, I lie down alone.

The horn[1] pillow so beautiful,
The worked coverlet so bright!
My lovely one is here no more.
With whom? No, alone I watch till dawn.

Summer days, winter nights—
Year after year of them must pass
Till I go to him where he dwells.
Winter nights, summer days—
Year after year of them must pass
Till I go to his home.

TWO SOLDIERS' SONGS

(I)

WHAT plant is not faded?
What day do we not march?
What man is not taken
To defend the four bounds?

[1] A pillow of wood, inlaid with horn.

What plant is not wilting?
What man is not taken from his wife?
Alas for us soldiers,
Treated as though we were not fellow-men!

Are we buffaloes, are we tigers
That our home should be these desolate wilds?
Alas for us soldiers,
Neither by day nor night can we rest!

The fox bumps and drags
Through the tall, thick grass.
Inch by inch move our barrows
As we push them along the track.

(2)

WE plucked the bracken, plucked the bracken
While the young shoots were springing up.
Oh, to go back, go back!
The year is ending.
We have no house, no home
Because of the Hsien-yün.
We cannot rest or bide
Because of the Hsien-yün.

We plucked the bracken, plucked the bracken
While the shoots were soft.
Oh, to go back, go back!
Our hearts are sad,
Our sad hearts burn,
We are hungry and thirsty,
But our campaign is not over,
Nor is any of us sent home with news.

We plucked the bracken, plucked the bracken;
But the shoots were hard.
Oh, to go back, go back!
The year is running out.
But the king's business never ends;
We cannot rest or bide.
Our hearts are very bitter;
We went, but do not come.

What splendid thing is that?
It is the flower of the cherry-tree.
What great carriage is that?
It is our lord's chariot,
His war-chariot ready yoked,
With its four steeds so eager.
How should we dare stop or tarry?
In one month we have had three alarms.

We yoke the teams of four,
Those steeds so strong,
That our lord rides behind,
That lesser men protect.
The four steeds so grand,
The ivory bow-ends, the fish-skin quiver.
Yes, we must be always on our guard;
The Hsien-yün are very swift.

Long ago, when we started,
The willows spread their shade.
Now that we turn back
The snowflakes fly.
The march before us is long,
We are thirsty and hungry,
Our hearts are stricken with sorrow,
But no one listens to our plaint.

RETURN FROM BATTLE

WIFE: Tall grows that pear-tree,
Its fruit so fair to see.[1]
The king's business never ends;
Day in, day out it claims us.

CHORUS: In spring-time, on a day so sunny—
Yet your heart full of grief?
The soldiers have leave!

---

[1] 'The tree flowers in its season but the soldiers cannot lead a natural existence' (earliest commentator). This use of contrast was completely misunderstood by later interpreters.

WIFE: Tall grows that pear-tree,
           Its leaves so thick.
           The king's business never ends;
           My heart is sick and sad.

CHORUS: Every plant and tree so leafy,
           Yet your heart sad?
           The soldiers are coming home!

SOLDIER: I climb that northern hill
           To pluck the boxthorn.
           The king's business never ends;
           What will become of my father, of my mother?

CHORUS: Their wickered chariots drag painfully along,
           Their horses are tired out.
           But the soldiers have not far to go.

WIFE: If he were not expected and did not come
           My heart would still be sad.
           But he named a day, and that day is passed,
           So that my torment is great indeed.

CHORUS: The tortoise and the yarrow-stalks agree;
           Both tell glad news.
           Your soldier is close at hand.

The tortoise and the yarrow-stalks represent two methods of divination. The first consisted in heating the carapace of a tortoise and 'reading' the cracks that appeared; the second, in shuffling stalks of the Siberian milfoil.

HERDSMAN'S SONG

WHO says you have no sheep?
Three hundred is the flock.
Who says you have no cattle?
Ninety are the black-lips.
Here your rams come,
Their horns thronging;
Here your cattle come,
Their ears flapping.

28

Some go down the slope,
Some are drinking in the pool,
Some are sleeping, some waking.
Here your herdsmen come
In rush-cloak and bamboo-hat,
Some shouldering their dinners.
Only thirty brindled[1] beasts!
Your sacrifices will not go short.

Your herdsman comes,
Bringing faggots, bringing brushwood,
With the cock-game, with hen-game.
Your rams come,
Sturdy and sound;
None that limps, none that ails.
He beckons to them with raised arm;
All go up into the stall.

Your herdsman dreams,
Dreams of locusts and fish,
Of banners and flags.
A wise man explains the dreams:
'Locusts and fishes
Mean fat years.
Flags and banners
Mean a teeming house and home.'[2]

DYNASTIC HYMN

So they appeared before their lord the king
To get from him their emblems,
Dragon-banners blazing bright,
Tuneful bells tinkling,
Bronze-knobbed reins jangling—
The gifts shone with glorious light.
Then they showed them to their shining ancestors
Piously, making offering,
That they might be vouchsafed long life,

[1] i.e. the rest are whole-coloured and therefore suitable for sacrifice.
[2] This helps to explain why flag-waving plays such a prominent part in the fertility-rites of peasant Europe.

Everlastingly be guarded.
Oh, a mighty store of blessings!
Glorious and mighty, those former princes and lords
Who secure us with many blessings,
Through whose bright splendours
We greatly prosper.

TWO LAMENTS

(1)

GINGERLY walked the hare,
But the pheasant was caught in the snare.
At the beginning of my life
All was still quiet;
In my latter days
I have met great calamities.[1]
Would that I might sleep and never stir!

Gingerly walked the hare;
But the pheasant got caught in the trap.
At the beginning of my life
The times were not yet troublous.
In my latter days
I have met great sorrows.
Would that I might sleep and wake no more!

Gingerly walked the hare;
But the pheasant got caught in the net.
At the beginning of my life
The times were still good.
In my latter days
I have met great disasters.
Would that I might sleep and hear no more!

(2)

OH, what has become of us?
Those big dish-stands that towered so high!

[1] The fall of the western Chou dynasty?

Today, even when we get food, there is none to spare.
Alas and alack!
We have not grown as we sprouted.

Oh, what has become of us?
Four dishes at every meal!
Today, even when we get food, there is never enough.
Alas and alack!
We have not grown as we sprouted.

THE BIG CHARIOT

DON'T help-on the big chariot;
You will only make yourself dusty.
Don't think about the sorrows of the world;
You will only make yourself wretched.

Don't help-on the big chariot;
You won't be able to see for dust.
Don't think about the sorrows of the world;
Or you will never escape from your despair.

Don't help-on the big chariot;
You'll be stifled with dust.
Don't think about the sorrows of the world;
You will only load yourself with care.

DANCE SONG

THE unicorn's hoofs!
The duke's sons throng.
Alas for the unicorn!

The unicorn's brow!
The duke's kinsmen throng.
Alas for the unicorn!

The unicorn's horn!
The duke's clansmen throng.
Alas for the unicorn!

31

HYMN TO THE FALLEN

(Fourth Century B.C. ?)

'WE hold our flat shields, we wear our jerkins of hide;
The axles of our chariots touch, our short swords meet.
Standards darken the sun, the foe roll on like clouds;
Arrows fall thick, the warriors press forward.
They have overrun our ranks, they have crossed our line;
The trace-horse on the left is dead, the one on the right is
    wounded.
The fallen horses block our wheels, our chariot is held fast;
We grasp our jade drum-sticks, we beat the rolling drums.'

Heaven decrees their fall, the dread Powers are angry;
The warriors are all dead, they lie in the open fields.
They set out, but shall not enter; they went but shall not
    come back.
The plains are empty and wide, the way home is long.
Their tall swords are at their waist, their bows are under
    their arm;
Though their heads were severed their spirit could not be
    subdued.
They that fought so well—in death are warriors still;
Stubborn and steadfast to the end, they could not be
    dishonoured.
Their bodies perished in the fight, but the magic of their
    souls is strong—
Captains among the ghosts, heroes among the Dead!

THE GREAT SUMMONS

Invocation to the soul of a dead or sick man.

Anon. (Third or Second Century B.C.)

GREEN Spring receiveth
The vacant earth;
The white sun shineth;
Spring wind provoketh
To burst and burgeon
Each sprout and flower.
The dark ice melts and moves; hide not, my soul!
O Soul come back again! O do not stray!

32

O Soul, come back again and go not east or west, or north
    or south!
For to the East a mighty water drowneth
    Earth's other shore;
Tossed on its waves and heaving with its tides
    The hornless Dragon of the Ocean rideth;
Clouds gather low and fogs enfold the sea
    And gleaming ice drifts past.
O Soul go not to the East,
To the silent Valley of Sunrise!

O Soul go not to the South
Where mile on mile the earth is burnt away
And poisonous serpents slither through the flames,
Where on precipitous paths or in deep woods
Tigers and leopards prowl,
And water-scorpions wait;
Where the king-python rears his giant head.
O Soul go not to the South
Where the three-footed tortoise spits disease!

O Soul go not to the West
Where level wastes of sand stretch on and on;
And demons rage, swine-headed, hairy-skinned,
With bulging eyes;
Who in wild laughter gnash projecting fangs.
O Soul go not to the West
Where many perils wait!

O Soul go not to the North,
To the Lame Dragon's frozen peaks;
Where trees and grasses dare not grow;
Where the river runs too wide to cross
And too deep to plumb,
And the sky is white with snow
And the cold cuts and kills.
O Soul seek not to fill
The treacherous voids of the North!

O Soul come back to idleness and peace.
In quietude enjoy
The lands of Ching and Ch'u.
There work your will and follow your desire

33

Till sorrow is forgot,
And carelessness shall bring you length of days.
O Soul come back to joys beyond all telling!

Where thirty cubits high at harvest-time
The corn is stacked;
Where pies are cooked of millet and water-grain,
Guests watch the steaming bowls
And sniff the pungency of peppered herbs.
The cunning cook adds slices of bird-flesh,
Pigeon and yellow-heron and black-crane.
They taste the badger-stew.
O Soul come back to feed on foods you love!

Next are brought
Fresh turtle, and sweet chicken cooked in cheese
Pressed by the men of Ch'u.
And pickled sucking-pig
And flesh of whelps floating in liver-sauce
With salad of minced radishes in brine;
All served with that hot spice of southernwood
The land of Wu supplies.
O Soul come back to choose the meats you love!

Roasted daw, steamed mallard and grilled quail—
On every fowl they fare.
Boiled perch and sparrow broth—in each preserved
The separate flavour that is most its own.
O Soul come back to where such dainties wait!

The four strong liquors are warming at the fire
So that they grate not on the drinker's throat.
How fragrant rise their fumes, how cool their taste!
Such drink is not for louts or serving-men!
And wise distillers from the land of Wu
Blend unfermented spirit with white yeast
And brew the _li_ of Ch'u.
O Soul come back and let your trembling cease!

Reed-organs from the lands of Tai and Ch'in
And Wei and Chêng
Gladden the feasters, and old songs are sung:
The 'Rider's Song' that once

Fu-hsi, the ancient monarch made;
And the shrill songs of Ch'u.
Then after prelude from the pipes of Chao
The ballad-singer's voice rises alone.
O Soul come back to the hollow mulberry-tree![1]

Eight and eight the dancers sway,
Weaving their steps to the poet's voice
Who speaks his odes and rhapsodies;
They tap their bells and beat their chimes
Rigidly, lest harp and flute
Should mar the measure.
Then rival singers of the Four Domains
Compete in melody, till not a tune
Is left unsung that human voice could sing.
O Soul come back and listen to their songs!

Then women enter whose red lips and dazzling teeth
Seduce the eye;
But meek and virtuous, trained in every art,
Fit sharers of play-time,
So soft their flesh and delicate their bones.
O Soul come back and let them ease your woe!

Then enter other ladies with laughing lips
And sidelong glances under moth eyebrows,
Whose cheeks are fresh and red;
Ladies both great of heart and long of limb,
Whose beauty by sobriety is matched.
Well-padded cheeks and ears with curving rim,
High-arching eyebrows, as with compass drawn,
Great hearts and loving gestures—all are there;
Small waists and necks as slender as the clasp
Of courtiers' buckles.
O Soul come back to those whose tenderness
Drives angry thoughts away!

Last enter those
Whose every action is contrived to please;
Black-painted eyebrows and white-powdered cheeks.
They reek with scent; with their long sleeves they brush
The faces of the feasters whom they pass,

[1] The lute.

Or pluck the coats of those who will not stay.
O Soul come back to pleasures of the night!

.   .   .   .

A summer-house with spacious rooms
And a high hall with beams stained red;
A little closet in the southern wing
Reached by a private stair.
And round the house a covered way should run
Where horses might be trained.

And sometimes riding, sometimes going afoot
You shall explore, O Soul, the parks of spring;
Your jewelled axles gleaming in the sun
And yoke inlaid with gold;
Or amid orchises and sandal-trees
Shall walk in the dark woods.
O Soul come back and live for these delights!

Peacocks shall fill your gardens; you shall rear
The rock and phoenix, and red jungle-fowl,
Whose cry at dawn assembles river storks
To join the play of cranes and ibises;
Where the wild-swan all day
Pursues the glint of idle kingfishers.
O Soul come back to watch the birds in flight!

He who has found such manifold delights
Shall feel his cheeks aglow
And the blood-spirit dancing through his limbs.
Stay with me, Soul, and share
The span of days that happiness will bring;
See sons and grandsons serving at the Court
Ennobled and enriched.
O Soul come back and bring prosperity
To house and stock!

The roads that lead to Ch'u
Shall teem with travellers as thick as clouds,
A thousand miles away.
For the Five Orders of Nobility
Shall summon sages to assist the King

And with godlike discrimination choose
The wise in council; by their aid to probe
The hidden discontents of humble men
And help the lonely poor.
O Soul come back and end what we began!

Fields, villages and lanes
Shall throng with happy men;
Good rule protect the people and make known
The King's benevolence to all the land;
Stern discipline prepare
Their natures for the soft caress of Art.
O Soul come back to where the good are praised!

Like the sun shining over the four seas
Shall be the reputation of our King;
His deeds, matched only in Heaven, shall repair
The wrongs endured by every tribe of men—
Northward to Yu and southward to Annam,
To the Sheep's-Gut Mountain and the Eastern Seas.
O Soul come back to where the wise are sought!

.   .   .   .

Behold the glorious virtues of our King
Triumphant, terrible;
Behold with solemn faces in the Hall
The three Grand Ministers walk up and down—
None chosen for the post save landed-lords
Or, in default, Knights of the Nine Degrees.
Clout and pin-hole are marked, already is hung
The shooting-target, where with bow in hand
And arrows under arm
Each archer does obeisance to each,
Willing to yield his rights of precedence.
O Soul come back to where men honour still
The name of the Three Kings.[1]

---

[1] Yü, T'ang and Wên, the three just rulers of antiquity.

THE AUTUMN WIND

By Wu-ti (157-87 B.C.), sixth emperor of the Han dynasty. He
came to the throne when he was only sixteen. In this poem he
regrets that he is obliged to go on an official journey, leaving
his mistress behind in the capital. He is seated in his state barge
surrounded by his ministers.

AUTUMN wind rises; white clouds fly.
Grass and trees wither; geese go south.
Orchids, all in bloom; chrysanthemums smell sweet;
I think of my lovely lady; I never can forget.
Floating-pagoda boat crosses Fên River;
Across the mid-stream white waves rise.
Flute and drum keep time to sound of rowers' song;
Amidst revel and feasting sad thoughts come;
Youth's years how few, age how sure!

LI FU-JÊN

THE sound of her silk skirt has stopped.
On the marble pavement dust grows.
Her empty room is cold and still.
Fallen leaves are piled against the doors.
      Longing for that lovely lady
How can I bring my aching heart to rest?

The above poem is supposed to have been written by Wu-ti
when his mistress, Li Fu-jên, died. Unable to bear his grief, he
sent for wizards from all parts of China, hoping that they would
be able to put him into communication with her spirit. At last
one of them managed to project her shape on to a curtain. The
emperor cried:

Is it or isn't it?
I stand and look.
The swish, swish of a silk skirt.
How slow she comes!

LAMENT OF HSI-CHÜN

About the year 105 B.C. a Chinese lady named Hsi-chün was
sent, for political reasons, to be the wife of a central Asian
nomad king, K'un Mo, king of the Wu-sun. When she got
there, she found her husband old and decrepit. He only saw
her once or twice a year, when they drank a cup of wine
together. They could not converse, as they had no language
in common.

MY people have married me
In a far corner of Earth;
Sent me away to a strange land,
To the king of the Wu-sun.
A tent is my house,
Of felt are my walls;
Raw flesh my food
With mare's milk to drink.
Always thinking of my own country,
My heart sad within.
Would I were a yellow stork
And could fly to my old home!

TO HIS WIFE

By General Su Wu (c. 100 B.C.)

SINCE my hair was plaited and we became man and wife
The love between us was never broken by doubt.
So let us be merry this night together,
Feasting and playing while the good time lasts.
I suddenly remember the distance that I must travel;
I spring from bed and look out to see the time.
The stars and planets are all grown dim in the sky;
Long, long is the road; I cannot stay.
I am going on service, away to the battle-ground,
And I do not know when I shall come back.
I hold your hand with only a deep sigh;
Afterwards, tears—in the days when we are parted.
With all your might enjoy the spring flowers,
But do not forget the time of our love and pride.
Know that if I live, I will come back again,
And if I die, we will go on thinking of each other.

39

PARTING FROM SU WU

By Li Ling

THE good time will never come back again;
In a moment our parting will be over.
Beside the cross-road we faltered, uneasily;
In the open fields we paused, hand in hand.
The clouds above are floating across the sky;
Swiftly, swiftly passing; or blending together.
The waves in the wind lose their fixed place
And are rolled away each to a corner of Heaven.
From now onwards long must be our parting,
So let us stop again for a little while.
I wish I could ride on the wings of the morning wind
And go with you right to your journey's end.

Li Ling and Su Wu were both prisoners in the land of the Huns. After nineteen years Su Wu was released. Li Ling would not go back with him. When invited to do so, he got up and danced, singing:

I CAME ten thousand leagues
Across sandy deserts
In the service of my Prince,
To break the Hun tribes.
My way was blocked and barred,
My arrows and sword broken.
My armies had faded away,
My reputation had gone.
My old mother is long dead.
Although I want to requite my Prince
How can I return?

POVERTY

By Yang Hsiung (52 B.C.-A.D. 18)

I, YANG TZŬ, hid from life,
Fled from the common world to a lonely place
Where to the right a great wilderness touched me
And on the left my neighbour was the Hill of Sung.
Beggars whose tenements
Lie wall to wall, though they be tattered and poor,

Rough-used, despised and scorned, are yet in companies
And sociable clans conjoined. But I in my despair
Called Poverty to me, saying: Long ago
You should have been cast out, driven far away,
Press-ganged, or pilloried as Man's fourth curse.
Yet not in childhood only, in infancy
When laughing I would build
Castles of soil or sand, were you
My more than neighbour, for your roof
Touched mine and our two homes were one;
But in manhood also weighed I with the great
Lighter because of you
Than fluff or feather; more frail my fortunes
Than gossamer, who to the State submitting
Great worth found small employ;
Withdrawing, heard no blame.

What prompts you, Poverty,
So long to linger, an unwanted guest?
Others wear broidered coats; my homespun is not whole.
Others eat millet and rice, I boil the goosefoot seed.
No toy nor treasure is mine,
Nor aught to make me glad.
Clans gather at the feast
In great ease and gladness,
But I abroad the world
Trudge out afoot with panniers on my back,
Sell my day-labour for a coat to cover me.
Servant of many masters
Hand-chafed I dig, heel-blistered hoe,
Bare-backed to the wind and rain.
And that all this befell me,
That friends and favourites forsook me,
That up the hill of State so laboured was my climb
Who should bear blame? Who but you, O Poverty,
Was cause of all my woe?

I fled you high and far, but you across the hills of heaven
Like a hawk did follow me.
I fled you among the rocks, in caverns of stone I hid;
But you up those huge steeps
Did follow me.
I fled you to the ocean, sailed that cypress ship

41

Across the storm, but you
Whether on wave-crest or in the hollows of the sea
Did follow me.
And if I move, you too are stirring;
If I lie down you are at rest.
Have you no other friend in all the world?
What would you seek of me?
Go, Poverty, and pester me no more.
Then said Poverty: So be it, my master;
I am dismissed. Yet though men say
'Much chatter, little wit', listen! I too
Have a heart that is full and a tale that must be told.

My father's father long, long ago
Was illustrious in the land, of virtue so excellent
That by the King's throne in council he stood
Admonishing the rulers how to make statutes and laws.
Of earth were the stairs, roofed over with thatch.
Not carved or hung.
But when the world in latter days
Was given over to folly, fell about in darkness,
Then gluttons gathered together; by ill means the covetous
Fastened upon their prey;
Despised my grand-dad, they were so insolent and proud,
Built arbours of onyx, terraces of jade,
And huge halls to dwell in, lapped lakes of wine.
So that at last I left them
Suddenly as a swan that soars
And would not tread their Court.
Thrice daily I look into my heart
And find I did no wrong.
As for your home, mighty are the blessings I brought,
Stacked high as the hills.
Your small woes you remember;
But my good deeds you have forgot.
Did I not teach you
By gradual usage, indifferent to endure
Summer's heat and winter's cold?
(And that which neither heat nor cold can touch—
Is it not eternal as the Gods?)

'I, Poverty,
Turned from you the envy of the covetous, taught you to fear

Neither Chieh the Tyrant nor the Robber Chih.
Others, my master,
Quake behind bolt and bar, while you alone
Live open to the world.
Others by care
And pitiful apprehension are cast down,
While you are gay and free.'
Thus spoke Poverty, and when his speech was ended,
Stern of countenance and with dilated eye,
He gathered up the folds of his garment and rose from
    where he sat,
Passed down the stairway and left my house.

'Farewell', said Poverty, 'for now I leave you.
To that hill I take my way
Where sheltering, the Lord of Ku-chu's sons
Have learnt to ply my trade.'
Then I, Yang Tzü, left the mat where I lay
And cried: 'O Poverty, let my crooked words
Be as unspoken; forget that I have wronged you.
I have heard truth, O Poverty, and received it.
Live with me always, for of your company
I shall not weary till I die.'
Then Poverty came back and lodged with me,
Nor since has left my side.

THE GOLDEN PALACE

Anon. (First Century A.D. ?)

WE go to the Golden Palace,
We set out jade cups,
We summon the honoured guests
To enter at the Golden Gate
And go to the Golden Hall.
In the Eastern Kitchen the meat is sliced and ready,
Pounded beef and boiled pork and mutton.
The Master of the Feast hands round the wine;
The lute-players sound the High Second.[1]
Some play darts, some face each other at chess;
The rival pieces are marshalled rank against rank.

[1] Name of a mode associated with songs of unhappy love.

43

The fire glows and the smoke puffs and curls,
From the incense-burner rises a delicate fragrance.
The clear wine has made our cheeks red;
Round the table joy and peace prevail.
May those who shared in this day's delight
Through countless autumns enjoy like felicity.

THE ORPHAN

Anon. (First Century A.D. ?)

To be an orphan,
To be fated to be an orphan,
How bitter is this lot!
When my father and mother were alive
I used to ride in a carriage
With four fine horses.
　　　But when they both died,
　　　My brother and my sister-in-law
　　　Sent me out to be a merchant.
In the south I travelled to the 'Nine Rivers'
And in the east as far as Ch'i and Lu.
At the end of the year when I came home
I dared not tell them what I had suffered—
Of the lice and vermin in my head,
Of the dust in my face and eyes.
My brother told me to get ready the dinner,
My sister-in-law told me to see after the horses.
I was always going up into the hall
And running down again to the parlour.
My tears fell like rain.
In the morning they sent me to draw water,
I didn't get back till night-fall,
My hands were all sore
And I had no shoes.
I walked the cold earth
Treading on thorns and brambles.
As I stopped to pull out the thorns,
How bitter my heart was!
My tears fell and fell
And I went on sobbing and sobbing.
In winter I have no great-coat;

44

Nor in summer thin clothes.
It is no pleasure to be alive.
I had rather quickly leave the earth
And go beneath the Yellow Springs.
The April winds blow
And the grass is growing green.
In the third month—silkworms and mulberries,
In the sixth month—the melon-harvest.
I went out with the melon-cart
And just as I was coming home
The melon-cart turned over.
The people who came to help me were few,
But the people who ate the melons were many.
'At least leave me the stalks
To take home as proof.
My brother and sister-in-law are harsh,
And will be certain to call me to account.'
When I got home, how they shouted and scolded!
I want to write a lettter and send it
To my mother and father under the earth,
And tell them I can't go on any longer
Living with my brother and sister-in-law.

'OLD POEM'

At fifteen I went with the army,
At fourscore I came home.
On the way I met a man from the village,
I asked him who there was at home.
'That over there is your house,
All covered over with trees and bushes.'
Rabbits had run in at the dog-hole,
Pheasants flew down from the beams of the roof
In the courtyard was growing some wild grain;
And by the well, some wild mallows.
I'll boil the grain and make porridge,
I'll pluck the mallows and make soup.
Soup and porridge are both cooked,
But there is no one to eat them with.
I went out and looked towards the east,
While tears fell and wetted my clothes.

45

MEETING IN THE ROAD

IN a narrow road where there was not room to pass
My carriage met the carriage of a young man.
And while his axle was touching my axle
In the narrow road I asked him where he lived.
'The place where I live is easy enough to find,
Easy to find and difficult to forget.
The gates of my house are built of yellow gold,
The hall of my house is paved with white jade,
On the hall table flagons of wine are set,
I have summoned to serve me dancers of Han-tan.[1]
In the midst of the courtyard grows a cassia-tree—
And candles on its branches flaring away in the night.'

FIGHTING SOUTH OF THE RAMPARTS

Anon. (First Century A.D. ?)

THEY fought south of the ramparts,
They died north of the wall.
They died in the moors and were not buried.
Their flesh was the food of crows.
'Tell the crows we are not afraid;
We have died in the moors and cannot be buried.
Crows, how can our bodies escape you?'
The waters flowed deep
And the rushes in the pool were dark.
The riders fought and were slain;
Their horses wander neighing.
By the bridge there was a house.[2]
Was it south, was it north?
The harvest was never gathered.
How can we give you your offerings?
You served your Prince faithfully,
Though all in vain.
I think of you, faithful soldiers;

[1] Capital of the kingdom of Chao, where the people were famous for
their beauty.
[2] There is no trace of it left. This passage describes the havoc of war.
The harvest has not been gathered: therefore corn-offerings cannot be
made to the spirits of the dead.

Your service shall not be forgotten.
For in the morning you went out to battle
And at night you did not return.

THE EASTERN GATE

Anon. (First Century A.D. ?)

A poor man determines to go out into the world and make his
fortune. His wife tries to detain him.

I WENT out at the eastern gate;
I never thought to return.
But I came back to the gate with my heart full of sorrow.
There was not a peck of rice in the bin;
There was not a coat hanging on the pegs.
So I took my sword and went towards the gate.
My wife and child clutched at my coat and wept;
'Some people want to be rich and grand;
I only want to share my porridge with you.
Above, we have the blue waves of the sky;
Below, the face of this child that suckles at my breast.'
     'Dear wife, I cannot stay.
     Soon it will be too late.
     When one is growing old
     One cannot put things off.'

OLD AND NEW

Anon. (First Century A.D. ?)

SHE went up the mountain to pluck wild herbs;
She came down the mountain and met her former husband.
She knelt down and asked her former husband
'What do you find your new wife like?'
'My new wife, although her talk is clever,
Cannot charm me as my old wife could.
In beauty of face there is not much to choose,
But in usefulness they are not at all alike.
My new wife comes in from the road to meet me;
My old wife always came down from her tower.
My new wife weaves fancy silks;

My old wife was good at plain weaving.
Of fancy silk one can weave a strip a day;
Of plain weaving, more than fifty feet.
Putting her silks by the side of your weaving
I see that the new will not compare with the old.'

SOUTH OF THE GREAT SEA

My love is living
To the south of the Great Sea.
What shall I send to greet him?
Two pearls and a comb of tortoise-shell:
I'll send them to him bound with ropes of jade.
They tell me he is not true;
They tell me he dashed my things to the ground,
Dashed them to the ground and burnt them
And scattered the ashes to the wind.
From this day to the ends of time
I must never think of him;
Never again think of him.
The cocks are crowing,
And the dogs are barking—
My brother and his wife will soon know.
The autumn wind is blowing;
The morning wind is sighing.
In a moment the sun will rise in the east
And then it too will know.

THE OTHER SIDE OF THE VALLEY

I am a prisoner in the hands of the enemy,
Enduring the shame of captivity.
My bones stick out and my strength is gone
Through not getting enough to eat.
My brother is a Mandarin
And his horses are fed on millet.
Why can't he spare a little money
To send and ransom me?

OATHS OF FRIENDSHIP

(1)

In the country of Yüeh when a man made friends with another
they set up an altar of earth and sacrificed upon it a dog and a
cock, reciting this oath as they did so:

> If you were riding in a coach
> And I were wearing a 'li',[1]
> And one day we met in the road,
> You would get down and bow.
> If you were carrying a 'tĕng'[2]
> And I were riding on a horse,
> And one day we met in the road
> I would get down for you.

(2)

> Shang Ya!
> I want to be your friend
> For ever and ever without break or decay.
> When the hills are all flat
> And the rivers are all dry,
> When it lightens and thunders in winter,
> When it rains and snows in summer,
> When Heaven and Earth mingle—
> Not till then will I part from you.

BURIAL SONGS

(1)

'The dew on the garlic-leaf', sung at the burial of kings and
princes.

> How swiftly it dries,
> The dew on the garlic-leaf,
> The dew that dries so fast
> Tomorrow will fall again.
> But he whom we carry to the grave
> Will never more return.

[1] A peasant's hat made of straw.
[2] An umbrella under which a cheap-jack sells his wares.

(2)

'The Graveyard', sung at the burial of common men.

> WHAT man's land is the graveyard?
> It is the crowded home of ghosts—
> Wise and foolish shoulder to shoulder.
> The King of the Dead claims them all;
> Man's fate knows no tarrying.

SEVENTEEN OLD POEMS

(First and Second Centuries A.D.)

(1)

> ON and on, always on and on
> Away from you, parted by a life-parting.[1]
> Going from one another ten thousand 'li',
> Each in a different corner of the World.
> The way between is difficult and long,
> Face to face how shall we meet again?
> The Tartar horse prefers the North wind,
> The bird from Yüeh nests on the Southern branch.
> Since we parted the time is already long,
> Daily my clothes hang looser round my waist.
> Floating clouds obscure the white sun,
> The wandering one has quite forgotten home.
> Thinking of you has made me suddenly old,
> The months and years swiftly draw to their close.
> That I'm cast away and rejected I must not repine;
> Better to hope that you eat your rice and thrive.

(2)

> GREEN, green,
> The grass by the river-bank.
> Thick, thick,
> The willow trees in the garden.
> Sad, sad,
> The lady in the tower.
> White, white,

[1] The opposite of a parting by death.

50

Sitting at the casement window.
Fair, fair,
Her red-powdered face.
Small, small,
She puts out her pale hand.
Once she was a dancing-house girl,
Now she is a wandering man's wife.
The wandering man went, but did not return.
It is hard alone to keep an empty bed.

(3)

GREEN, green,
The cypress on the mound.
Firm, firm,
The boulder in the stream.
Man's life lived within this world
Is like the sojourning of a hurried traveller.
A cup of wine together will make us glad,
And a little friendship is no little matter.

Yoking my chariot I urge my stubborn horses,
I wander about in the streets of Wan and Lo.[1]
In Lo Town how fine everything is!
The 'Caps and Belts'[2] go seeking each other out.
The great boulevards are intersected by lanes,
Wherein are the town-houses of Royal Dukes.
The two palaces stare at each other from afar,
The twin gates rise a hundred feet.
By prolonging the feast let us keep our hearts gay,
And leave no room for sadness to creep in.

(4)

OF this day's glorious feast and revel
The pleasure and delight are difficult to describe.
Plucked from the lute in a swift, tumultuous jangling
The new melodies in beauty reached the divine.
Skilful singers intoned the high words,
Those who knew the tune heard the trueness of their
    singing.

[1] Nan-yang and Lo-yang, in Honan.   [2] High officers.

We sat there each with the same desire
And like thoughts by each unexpressed:
'Man in the world lodging for a single lifetime
Passes suddenly like dust borne on the wind.
Then let us hurry out with high steps
And be the first to reach the highways and fords,
Rather than stay at home wretched and poor,
For long years plunged in sordid grief.'

(5)

In the north-west there is a high house,
Its top level with the floating clouds.
Embroidered curtains thinly screen its windows
Its storeyed tower is built on three steps.
From above there comes a noise of playing and singing,
The tune sounding, oh how sad!
Who can it be, playing so sad a tune?
Surely it must be Ch'i Liang's wife.[1]
The High Second[2] follows the wind's rising,
The middle lay lingers indecisive.
To each note, two or three sobs,
Her high will conquered by overwhelming grief.
She does not regret that she is left so sad,
But minds that so few can understand her song.
She wants to become those two wild geese
That with beating wings rise high aloft.

(6)

Crossing the river I pluck the lotus flowers;
In the orchid-swamps are many fragrant herbs.
I gather them, but who shall I send them to?
My love is living in lands far away.
I turn and look towards my own country;
The long road stretches on for ever.
The same heart, yet a different dwelling:
Always fretting, till we are grown old!

[1] Who wailed so loud when her husband failed to return from battle
that she brought down the city-wall.   [2] See above, p. 43.

7

A BRIGHT moon illumines the night-prospect;
The house-cricket chirrups on the eastern wall.
The Handle of the Pole-star points to the Beginning of
      Winter;
The host of stars is scattered over the sky.
The white dew wets the moor-grasses—
With sudden swiftness the times and seasons change.
The autumn cicada sings among the trees,
The swallows, alas, whither are they gone?
Once I had a same-house friend,
He took flight and rose high away.
He did not remember how once we went hand in hand,
But left me like footsteps behind one in the dust.
In the South is the Winnowing-fan and the Pole-star in
      the North,
And a Herd-boy[1] whose ox has never borne the yoke.
A friend who is not firm as a great rock
Is of no profit and idly bears the name.

8

IN the courtyard there grows a strange tree,
Its green leaves ooze with a fragrant moisture.
Holding the branch I cut a flower from the tree,
Meaning to send it away to the person I love.
Its sweet smell fills my sleeves and lap.
The road is long, how shall I get it there?
Such a thing is not fine enough to send;
But it may remind him of the time that has passed since
      he left.[2]

FAR away twinkles the Herd-boy star;
Brightly shines the Lady of the Han River.
Slender, slender she plies her white fingers;
Click, click go the wheels of her spinning loom.

[1] Name of a star. The Herd-boy, who is only figuratively speaking a
herd-boy, is like the friend who is no real friend.
[2] i.e. (supposing he went away in the autumn) remind him that spring
has come.

At the end of the day she has not finished her task;
Her bitter tears fall like streaming rain.
The Han River runs shallow and clear;
Set between them, how short a space!
But the river water will not let them pass,
Gazing at each other but never able to speak.

(10)

TURNING my chariot I yoke my horses and go.
On and on down the long roads
The autumn winds shake the hundred grasses.
On every side, how desolate and bare!
The things I meet are all new things,
Their strangeness hastens the coming of old age.
Prosperity and decay each have their season;
Success is bitter when it is slow in coming.
Man's life is not metal or stone,
He cannot far prolong the days of his fate.
Suddenly he follows in the way of things that change;
Fame is the only treasure that endures.

(11)

THE Eastern Wall stands high and long;
Far and wide it stretches without a break.
The whirling wind uprises and shakes the earth;
The autumn grasses grow thick and green.
The four seasons alternate without pause,
The year's end hurries swiftly on.
The Bird of the Morning Wind is stricken with sorrow;
The frail cicada suffers and is hard pressed.
Free and clear, let us loosen the bonds of our hearts.
Why should we go on always restraining and binding?
In Yen and Chao are many fair ladies,
Beautiful people with faces like jade.
Their clothes are made all of silk gauze,
They stand at the door practising shrill lays.
The echo of their singing, how sad it sounds!
By the pitch of the song one knows the stops have been
    tightened.
To ease their minds they arrange their shawls and belts;

Lowering their song, a little while they pause.
'I should like to be those two flying swallows
Who are carrying clay to nest in the eaves of your house.'

(12)

I DRIVE my chariot up to the Eastern Gate;
From afar I see the graveyard north of the Wall.
The white aspens how they murmur, murmur;
Pines and cypresses flank the broad paths.
Beneath lie men who died long ago;
Black, black is the long night that holds them.
Deep down beneath the Yellow Springs,
Thousands of years they lie without waking.

In infinite succession light and darkness shift,
And years vanish like the morning dew.
Man's life is like a sojourning,
His longevity lacks the firmness of stone and metal.
For ever it has been that mourners in their turn were
　　　mourned,
Saint and Sage—all alike are trapped.
Seeking by food to obtain immortality
Many have been the dupe of strange drugs.
Better far to drink good wine
And clothe our bodies in robes of satin and silk.

(13) CONTINUATION OF (12)

The dead are gone and with them we cannot converse;
The living are here and ought to have our love.
Leaving the city gate I look ahead
And see before me only mounds and tombs.
The old graves are ploughed up into fields,
The pine and cypresses are hewn for timber.
In the white aspens sad winds sing;
Their long murmuring kills my heart with grief.
I want to go home, to ride to my village gate;
I want to go back, but there's no road back.

(14)

THE years of a lifetime do not reach a hundred,
Yet they contain a thousand years' sorrow.
When days are short and the dull nights long,
Why not take a lamp and wander forth?
If you want to be happy you must do it now,
There is no waiting till an after-time.
The fool who's loath to spend the wealth he's got
Becomes the laughing-stock of after ages.
It is true that Master Wang[1] became immortal,
But how can *we* hope to share his lot?

(15)

COLD, cold the year draws to its end,
The mole-cricket makes a doleful chirping.
The chill wind increases its violence.
My wandering love has no coat to cover him.
He gave his embroidered furs to the Lady of Lo,[2]
But from me his bedfellow he is quite estranged.
Sleeping alone in the depth of the long night
In a dream I thought I saw the light of his face.
My dear one thought of our old joys together,
He came in his chariot and gave me the front reins.
I wanted so to prolong our play and laughter,
To hold his hand and go back with him in his coach.
But when he had come he would not stay long
Nor stop to go with me to the Inner Chamber.
Truly without the falcon's wings to carry me
How can I rival the flying wind's swiftness?
I go and lean at the gate and think of my grief,
My falling tears wet the double gates.

(16)

AT the beginning of winter a cold spirit comes,
The North Wind blows—chill, chill.
My sorrows being many, I know the length of the nights,
Raising my head I look at the stars in their places.
On the fifteenth day the bright moon is full,

---

[1] Who ascended to Heaven on a white crane.   [2] See below, p. 58.

On the twentieth day the 'toad and hare' wane.[1]
A stranger came to me from a distant land
And brought me a single scroll with writing on it;
At the top of the scroll was written 'Do not forget',
At the bottom was written 'Good-bye for ever'.
I put the letter away in the folds of my dress,
For three years the writing did not fade.
How with an undivided heart I loved you
I fear that you will never know or guess.

(17)

THE bright moon, oh how white it shines,
Shines down on the gauze curtains of my bed!
Racked by sorrow I toss and cannot sleep;
Picking up my clothes, I wander up and down.
My absent love says that he is happy,
But I would rather he said he was coming back.
Out in the courtyard I stand hesitating, alone;
To whom can I tell the sad thoughts I think?
Staring before me I enter my room again;
Falling tears wet my mantle and robe.

SONG OF THE SNOW-WHITE HEADS

Anon. (First Century A.D. ?)

OUR love was pure
As the snow on the mountains;
White as a moon
Between the clouds—
They're telling me
Your thoughts are double;
That's why I've come
To break it off.
Today we'll drink
A cup of wine.
Tomorrow we'll part
Beside the Canal:
Walking about

[1] The 'toad and hare' correspond to our 'man in the moon'. The waning of the moon symbolizes the waning of the lover's affection.

57

Beside the Canal,
Where its branches divide
East and west.
Alas and alas,
And again alas.
So must a girl
Cry when she's married,
If she find not a man
Of single heart,
Who will not leave her
Till her hair is white.

THE SONG OF LO-FU

Anon. (First Century A.D. ?)

THE sun has risen on the eastern brim of the world,
Shines into the high chambers of the house of Ch'in.
In the house of Ch'in is a lovely lady dwelling,
That calls herself the Lady Lo-fu.
This lady loves her silk-worms and mulberry-trees;
She's plucking leaves at the southern corner of the walls.
With blue thread are the joints of her basket bound;
Of cassia-boughs are the loops of her basket made.
Her soft hair hangs in loose plaits;
The pearl at her ear shines like a dazzling moon.
Of yellow damask is made her skirt beneath;
Of purple damask is made her coat above.
The passer-by who looks on Lo-fu
Drops his luggage and twirls his beard and moustache.
The young men when they see Lo-fu
Doff their caps and tie their filets on their brows.
The labouring ploughman thinks no more of his plough,
The hind in the field thinks no more of his hoe.
When they come home there is temper on both sides:
'You sat all day looking at Lo-fu!'
The Lord Prefect drives his coach from the south;
His five horses suddenly show their pace.
He's sent his officer: 'Quickly bring me word
Of what house may this lovely lady be?'
'In the house of Ch'in the fair lady dwells;
She calls herself the Lady Lo-fu.'

'Oh tell me, officer, tell me how old she may be!'
'A score of years she has not yet filled;
To fifteen she has added somewhat more.'
The Lord Prefect sends to Lo-fu:
'Tell me, lady, will you ride by me or no?'
She stands before him, she gives him answer straight:
'My Lord Prefect has not ready wits.
Has he not guessed that just as he has a wife
So I too have my husband dear?
Yonder to eastward a band of horse is riding,
More than a thousand, and my love is at their head.'
'By what sign shall I your husband know?'
'His white horse is followed by a black colt,
With blue thread is tied the horse's tail;
With yellow gold is bridled that horse's head.
At his waist he wears a windlass-hilted sword
You could not buy for many pounds of gold.
At fifteen they made him the Prefect's clerk;
At twenty they made him a Captain of the Guard.
At thirty he sat at the Emperor's Council Board,
At forty they gave him a city for his very own—[1]
A wholesome man, fair, white and fine;
Very hairy, with a beard that is thick and long.
Proudly and proudly he walks to his palace gate;
Stately, stately he strides through his palace hall.
In that great hall thousands of followers sit,
Yet none but names him the finest man of them all.'

THE BONES OF CHUANG TZU[2]

By CHANG HÊNG (A.D. 78-139)

I, CHANG P'ING-TZU, had traversed the Nine Wilds and
    seen their wonders,
In the eight continents beheld the ways of Man,
The Sun's procession, the orbit of the Stars,
The surging of the dragon, the soaring of the phoenix in
    his flight.
In the red desert to the south I sweltered,

[1] He became Prefect of a city.
[2] The great Taoist philosopher, see my *Three Ways of Thought in Ancient China*, 1939.

And northward waded through the wintry burghs of Yu.
Through the Valley of Darkness to the west I wandered,
And eastward travelled to the Sun's abode,
The stooping Mulberry Tree.

So the seasons sped; weak autumn languished,
A small wind woke the cold.
And now with rearing of rein-horse,
Plunging of the tracer, round I fetched
My high-roofed chariot to westward.
Along the dykes we loitered, past many meadows,
And far away among the dunes and hills.
Suddenly I looked and by the roadside
I saw a man's bones lying in the squelchy earth,
Black rime-frost over him; and I in sorrow spoke
And asked him, saying, 'Dead man, how was it?
Fled you with your friend from famine and for the last grains
Gambled and lost? Was this earth your tomb,
Or did floods carry you from afar? Were you mighty,
    were you wise,
Were you foolish and poor? A warrior, or a girl?'
Then a wonder came; for out of the silence a voice—
Thin echo only, in no substance was the Spirit seen—
Mysteriously answered, saying, 'I was a man of Sung,
Of the clan of Chuang; Chou was my name.
Beyond the climes of common thought
My reason soared, yet could I not save myself;
For at the last, when the long charter of my years was told,
I, too, for all my magic, by Age was brought
To the Black Hill of Death.
Wherefore, O Master, do you question me?'
Then I answered:
'Let me plead for you upon the Five Hill-tops,
Let me pray for you to the Gods of Heaven and the Gods
    of Earth,
That your white bones may arise,
And your limbs be joined anew.
The God of the North shall give me back your ears;
I will scour the Southland for your eyes.
From the sunrise I will wrest your feet;
The West shall yield your heart.
I will set each several organ in its throne;
Each subtle sense will I restore.

Would you not have it so?'
The dead man answered me:
'O Friend, how strange and unacceptable your words!
In death I rest and am at peace; in life, I toiled and strove.
Is the hardness of the winter stream
Better than the melting of spring?
All pride that the body knew
Was it not lighter than dust?
What Ch'ao and Hsü despised,
What Po-ch'êng fled,
Shall I desire, whom death
Already has hidden in the Eternal Way—
Where Li Chu cannot see me,
Nor Tzŭ Yeh hear me,
Where neither Yao nor Shun can reward me,
Nor the tyrants Chieh and Hsin condemn me,
Leopard nor tiger harm me,
Lance prick me nor sword wound me?
Of the Primal Spirit is my substance; I am a wave
In the river of Darkness and Light.
The Maker of All Things is my Father and Mother,
Heaven is my bed and earth my cushion,
The thunder and lightning are my drum and fan,
The sun and moon my candle and my torch,
The Milky Way my moat, the stars my jewels.
With Nature my substance is joined;
I have no passion, no desire.
Wash me and I shall be no whiter,
Foul me and I shall yet be clean.
I come not, yet am here;
Hasten not, yet am swift.'
The voice stopped, there was silence.
A ghostly light
Faded and expired.
I gazed upon the dead, stared in sorrow and compassion.
Then I called upon my servant that was with me
To tie his silken scarf about those bones
And wrap them in a cloak of sombre dust;
While I, as offering to the soul of this dead man,
Poured my hot tears upon the margin of the road.

THE DANCERS OF HUAI-NAN

(A Fragment)

By CHANG HÊNG

I saw them dancing at Huai-nan and made this poem of praise:

THE instruments of music are made ready,
Strong wine is in our cups;
Flute-songs flutter, to a din of magic drums.
Sound scuds and scatters, surges free as a flood. . . .
And now when the drinkers were all drunken,
And the sun had fallen to the west,
Up rose the fair ones to the dance,
Well painted and apparelled,
In veils of soft gossamer
All wound and meshed;
And ribbons they unravelled,
And scarfs to bind about their heads.
The wielder of the little stick
Whispers them to their places, and the steady drums
Draw them through the mazes of the dance.
They have raised their long sleeves, they have covered
　　their eyes;
Slowly their shrill voices
Swell the steady song.
And the song said:
As a frightened bird whose love
Has wandered away from the nest,
I flutter my desolate wings.
For the wind blows back to my home,
And I long for my father's house.

Subtly from slender hips they swing,
Swaying, slanting delicately up and down.
And like the crimson lotus flower
Glows their beauty, shedding flames afar.
They lift languid glances,
Peep distrustfully, till of a sudden
Ablaze with liquid light
Their soft eyes kindle. So dance to dance
Endlessly they weave, break off and dance again.
Now flutter their skirts like a great bird in flight,
Now toss their long white sleeves like whirling snow.

So the hours go by, till at last
The powder has blown from their cheeks, the black
    from their brows,
Flustered now are the fair faces, pins of pearl
Torn away, tangled the black tresses.
With combs they catch and gather in
The straying locks, put on the gossamer gown
That trailing winds about them, and in unison
Of body, song and dress, obedient
Each shadows each, as they glide softly to and fro.

THE LYCHEE-TREE

(Fragment)

By WANG I (c. A.D. 120)

SOMBRE as the heavens when morning clouds arise,
Bushy as a great broom held across the sky,
Vast as the spaces of a lofty house,
Deep fretted as a line of stony hills.
Long branches twining,
Green leaves clustering,
And all a-glimmer like a mist that lightly lies
Across the morning sun;
All spangled, darted with fire like a sky
Of populous stars.
Shell like a fisherman's red net;
Fruit white and lustrous as a pearl . . .
Lambent as the jewel of Ho, more strange
Than the saffron-stone of Hsia.
Now sigh we at the beauty of its show,
Now triumph in its taste.
Sweet juices lie in the mouth,
Soft scents invade the mind.
All flavours here are joined, yet none is master;
A hundred diverse tastes
Blend in such harmony no man can say
That one outstrips the rest. Sovereign of sweets,
Peerless, pre-eminent fruit, who dwellest apart
In noble solitude!

THE WANGSUN[1]

By WANG YEN-SHOU, SON OF WANG I (*c.* A.D. 130)

SUBLIME was he, stupendous in invention,
Who planned the miracles of earth and sky.
Wondrous the power that charged
Small things with secret beauty, moving in them all.
See now the wangsun, crafty creature, mean of size,
Uncouth of form; the wrinkled face
Of an aged man; the body of a little child.
See how in turn he blinks and blenches with an air
Pathetically puzzled, dimly gazes
Under tired lids, through languid lashes
Looks tragic and hollow-eyed, rumples his brow,
Scatters this way and that
An insolent, astonished glare;
Sniffs and snorts, snuffs and sneezes,
Snicks and cocks his knowing little ears!
Now like a dotard mouths and chews
Or hoots and hisses through his pouted lips;
Shows gnashing teeth, grates and grinds ill-temperedly,
Gobbles and puffs and scolds.
And every now and then,
Down to his belly, from the larder that he keeps
In either cheek, he sends
Little consignments lowered cautiously.
Sometimes he squats
Like a puppy on its haunches, or hare-like humps
An arching back;
Smirks and wheedles with ingratiating sweetness;
Or suddenly takes to whining, surly snarling;
Then, like a ravening tiger roars.

He lives in thick forests, deep among the hills,
Or houses in the clefts of sharp, precipitous rocks;
Alert and agile is his nature, nimble are his wits;
Swift are his contortions,
Apt to every need,
Whether he climb tall tree-stems of a hundred feet,
Or sways on the shuddering shoulder of a long bough,
Before him, the dark gullies of unfathomable streams;

---

[1] A kind of small, tailless ape (?).

64

Behind, the silent hollows of the lonely hills.
Twigs and tendrils are his rocking-chairs,
On rungs of rotting wood he trips
Up perilous places; sometimes, leap after leap,
Like lightning flits through the woods.
Sometimes he saunters with a sad, forsaken air;
Then suddenly peeps round
Beaming with satisfaction. Up he springs,
Leaps and prances, whoops, and scampers on his way.
Up cliffs he scrambles, up pointed rocks,
Dances on shale that shifts or twigs that snap,
Suddenly swerves and lightly passes. . . .
Oh, what tongue could unravel
The tale of all his tricks?

Alas, one trait
With the human tribe he shares; their sweet's his sweet,
Their bitter is his bitter. Off sugar from the vat
Or brewer's dregs he loves to sup.
So men put wine where he will pass.
How he races to the bowl!
How nimbly licks and swills!
Now he staggers, feels dazed and foolish,
Darkness falls upon his eyes. . . .
He sleeps and knows no more.
Up steal the trappers, catch him by the mane,
Then to a string or ribbon tie him, lead him home;
Tether him in the stable or lock him into the yard;
Where faces all day long
Gaze, gape, gasp at him and will not go away.

THE NIGHTMARE

By WANG YEN-SHOU

One night, about the time I came of age, I dreamt that demon
creatures fought with me while I slept. . . . When I woke I told
this vision in verse, that the dreamers of posterity might use my
poem as a spell to drive off evil dreams. And so often has it
proved its worth that I dare not any longer hide it from the
world. The words are these:

ONCE, as in the darkness I lay asleep by night,
Strange things suddenly saw I in my dream;

65

All my dream was of monsters that came about me
    while I slept,
Devils and demons, four-horned, serpent-necked,
Fishes with bird-tails, three-legged bogies
From six eyes staring; dragons hideous,
Yet three-part human.
On rushed the foul flocks, grisly legions,
Stood round me, stretched out their arms,
Danced their hands about me, and sought to snatch me
    from my bed.
Then cried I (and in my dream
My voice was thick with anger and my words all awry),
'Ill-spawned elves, how dare you
Beset with your dire shapes Creation's cleanest
Shapeliest creature, Man?' Then straightway I struck
    out,
Flashed my fists like lightning among them, thumped
    like thunder,
Here slit Jack-o'-Lantern,
Here smashed fierce Hog-Face,
Battered wights and goblins,
Smote venturous vampires, pounded in the dust
Imps, gnomes and lobs,
Kobolds and kelpies;
Swiped bulge-eyed bogies, oafs and elves;
Clove Tough-head's triple skull, threw down
Clutching Night-hag, flogged the gawky Ear-wig Fiend
That floundered toward me on its tail.

I struck at staring eyes,
Stamped on upturned faces; through close ranks
Of hoofs I cut my way, buried my fingers deep
In half-formed flesh;
Ghouls tore at my touch; I slit sharp noses,
Trod on red tongues, seized shaggy manes,
Shook bald-heads by the beard.
Then was a scuffling. Arms and legs together
Chasing, crashing and sliding; a helter-skelter
Of feet lost and found in the tugging and toppling,
Cuffing, cudgelling, frenzied flogging. . . .

So fought I, till terror and dismay
Shook those foul flocks; panic spread like a flame

Down mutinous ranks; they stand, they falter,
Those ghastly legions; but fleeing, suddenly turn
Glazed eyes upon me, to see how now I fare.
At last, to end their treachery
Again I rushed upon them, braved their slaver and
  snares,
Stood on a high place, and lashed down among them,
Shrieking and cursing as my blows crashed.
Then three by three and four by four
One after another hop-a-trot they fled,
Bellowing and bawling till the air was full of their
  breath—
Grumbling and snarling,
Those vanquished ogres, demons discomfited,
Some that would fain have run
Lolling and lurching, some that for cramped limbs
Could not stir from where they stood. Some over belly-
  wounds
Bent double; some in agony gasping and groaning.
Suddenly the clouds broke and (I knew not why)
A thin light filtered the darkness; then, while again
I sighed in wonder that those disastrous creatures,
Dire monstrosities, should dare assail
A clean and comely man, . . . there sounded in my ears
A twittering and crowing. And outdoors it was light.
The noisy cock, mindful that dawn was in the sky,
Had crowed his warning, and the startled ghosts,
Because they heard dawn heralded, had fled
In terror and tribulation from the rising day.

(In an epilogue the poet seeks consolation in the fact that
many evil dreams and occurrences have in the past been
omens of good. Duke Huan of Ch'i, while hunting in the
marshes, saw in a vision an ogre 'as broad as a cartwheel and as
long as a shaft, wearing a purple coat and red cap'. It was an
omen that he would rise to the Pentarchy. Wu Ting, Emperor
of the Shang dynasty, was haunted in a dream by the face of the
man who afterwards became his wise counsellor and friend.
Wên, Duke of Chin, dreamt that the Marquis of Ch'u held
him prostrate and sucked out his brains; yet his kingdom
defeated Ch'u. Lao Tzŭ made use of demons, and thereby
became leader among the Spirits of Heaven. 'So evil turns to
good.')

TO HIS WIFE

Ch'in Chia (*c.* A.D. 147) was summoned to take up an appointment at the capital at a time when his wife was ill and staying with her parents. He was therefore unable to say goodbye to her, and sent her three poems instead. This is the last of the three.

> SOLEMN, solemn the coachman gets ready to go;
> 'Chiang, chiang' the harness bells ring.
> At break of dawn I must start on my long journey;
> At cock-crow I must gird on my belt.
> I turn back and look at the empty room;
> For a moment I almost think I see you there.
> One parting, but ten thousand regrets;
> As I take my seat, my heart is unquiet.
> What shall I do to tell you all my thoughts?
> How can I let you know of all my love?
> Precious hairpins make the head to shine
> And bright mirrors can reflect beauty.
> Fragrant herbs banish evil smells
> And the scholar's lute has a clear note.
> The man in the Book of Songs[1] who was given a quince
> Wanted to pay it back with precious stones.
> When I think of all the things you have done for me,
> How ashamed I am to have done so little for you!
> Although I know that it is a poor return,
> All I can give you is this description of my feelings.

CH'IN CHIA'S WIFE'S REPLY

> MY poor body is alas unworthy;
> I was ill when first you brought me home.
> Limp and weary in the house—
> Time passed and I got no better.
> We could hardly ever see each other;
> I could not serve you as I ought.
> Then you received the Imperial Mandate;
> You were ordered to go far away to the City.
> Long, long must be our parting;
> I was not destined to tell you thoughts.

[1] See my *The Book of Songs*, p. 31.

I stood on tiptoe gazing into the distance,
Interminably gazing at the road that had taken you.
With thoughts of you my mind is obsessed;
In my dreams I see the light of your face.
Now you are started on your long journey
Each day brings you further from me.
Oh that I had a bird's wings
And high flying could follow you.
Long I sob and long I cry;
The tears fall down and wet my skirt.

ON THE DEATH OF HIS FATHER

By WEI WÊN-TI, son of Ts'ao Ts'ao, who founded the dynasty
of Wei, and died in A.D. 220.

I LOOK up and see his curtains and bed;
I look down and examine his table and mat.
The things are there just as before;
But the man they belonged to is not there.
His spirit suddenly has taken flight
And left me behind far away.
To whom shall I look, on whom rely?
My tears flow in an endless stream.
'Yu, yu' cry the wandering deer
As they carry fodder to their young in the wood.
Flap, flap fly the birds
As they carry their little ones back to the nest.
I alone am desolate
Dreading the days of our long parting;
My grieving heart's settled pain
No one else can understand.
There is a saying among people
'Sorrow makes us grow old.'
Alas, alas for my white hairs!
All too early they have come!
Long wailing, long sighing
My thoughts are fixed on my sage parent.
They say the good live long;
Then why was he not spared?

THE RUINS OF LO-YANG

By Ts'AO CHIH (A.D. 192-232), third son of Ts'ao Ts'ao. He was a great favourite with his father till he made a mistake in a campaign. This is one of two poems of farewell to a friend who was going north. Lo-yang was sacked by rebels in A.D. 190.

I CLIMB to the ridge of the Pei-mang Hills
And look down on the city of Lo-yang.
In Lo-yang how still it is!
Palaces and houses all burnt to ashes.
Walls and fences all broken and gaping,
Thorns and brambles shooting up to the sky.
I do not see the old old-men;
I only see the new young men.
I turn aside, for the straight road is lost;
The fields are overgrown and will never be ploughed
      again.
I have been away such a long time
That I do not know which path is which.
How sad and ugly the empty moors are!
A thousand miles without the smoke of a chimney.
I think of our life together all those years;
My heart is tied with sorrow and I cannot speak.

THE COCK-FIGHT

By Ts'AO CHIH

OUR wandering eyes are sated with the dancer's skill,
Our ears are weary with the sound of 'kung' and
      'shang'.[1]
Our host is silent and sits doing nothing;
All the guests go on to places of amusement.

.   .   .   .

On long benches the sportsmen sit ranged
Round a cleared room, watching the fighting-cocks.
The gallant birds are all in battle-trim;
They raise their tails and flap defiantly.
Their beating wings stir the calm air;
Their angry eyes gleam with a red light.

[1] Notes of the scale.

Where their beaks have struck, the fine feathers are
    scattered;
With their strong talons they wound again and again.
Their long cries enter the blue clouds;
Their flapping wings tirelessly beat and throb.
'Pray God the lamp-oil lasts a little longer,
Then I shall not leave without winning the match!'

A VISION

By Ts'ao Chih

In the Nine Provinces there is not room enough;
I want to soar high among the clouds,
And, far beyond the Eight Limits of the compass,
Cast my gaze across the unmeasured void.
I will wear as my gown the red mists of sunrise
And as my skirt the white fringes of the clouds;
My canopy—the dim lustre of Space,
My chariot—six dragons mounting heavenward;
And before the light of Time has shifted a pace
Suddenly stand upon the World's blue rim.
The doors of Heaven swing open,
The double gates shine with a red light.
I roam and linger in the palace of Wên-ch'ang,
I climb up to the hall of T'ai-wei.
The Lord God lies at his western lattice;
And the lesser Spirits are together in the eastern gallery.
They wash me in a bath of rainbow-spray
And gird me with a belt of jasper and rubies.
I wander at my ease gathering divine herbs;
I bend down and touch the scented flowers.
Wang-tzŭ[1] gives me drugs of long-life
And Hsien-mên[1] hands me strange potions.
By the partaking of food I evade the rites of Death;
My span is extended to the enjoyment of life everlasting.

[1] Names of Immortals.

THE LIBERATOR

A Political Allegory

By Ts'ao Chih

IN the high trees—many doleful winds;
The ocean waters—lashed into waves.
If the sharp sword be not in your hand,
How can you hope your friends will remain many?
Do you not see that sparrow on the fence?
Seeing the hawk it casts itself into the snare.
The fowler to catch the sparrow is delighted;
The Young Man to see the sparrow is grieved.
He takes his sword and cuts through the netting;
The yellow sparrow flies away, away.
Away, away, up to the blue sky
And down again to thank the Young Man.

THE CURTAIN OF THE WEDDING BED

By LIU HSÜN'S WIFE (Third Century A.D.)

After she had been married to him for a long while, General
Liu Hsün sent his wife back to her home, because he had
fallen in love with a girl of the Ssu-ma family.

FLAP, flap, you curtain in front of our bed!
I hung you there to screen us from the light of day.
I brought you with me when I left my father's house;
Now I am taking you back with me again.
I will fold you up and lay you flat in your box.
Curtain—shall I ever take you out again?

BEARER'S SONG

By MIU HSI (A.D. 186-245). Cf. the *Han Burial Songs*, p. 55

WHEN I was alive, I wandered in the streets of the Capital;
Now that I am dead, I am left to lie in the fields.
In the morning I drove out from the High Hall;
In the evening I lodged beneath the Yellow Springs.[1]

[1] Hades.

When the white sun had sunk in the Western Chasm
I hung up my chariot and rested my four horses.
Now, even the mighty Maker of All
Could not bring the life back to my limbs.
Shape and substance day by day will vanish:
Hair and teeth will gradually fall away.
For ever from of old men have been so:
And none born can escape this thing.

REGRET

By Yüan Chi (A.D. 210-263)

When I was young I learnt fencing
And was better at it than Ch'ü-ch'êng.[1]
My spirit was high as the rolling clouds
And my fame resounded beyond the World.
I took my sword to the desert sands,
I watered my horse in the Nine Wilds.
My flags and banners flapped in the wind,
And nothing was heard but the song of my drums.

War and its travels have made me sad,
And a fierce anger burns within me.
It's thinking of how I've wasted my time
That makes this fury tear my heart.

TAOIST SONG

By Hsi K'ang (A.D. 223-262)

I will cast out Wisdom and reject Learning;
My thoughts shall wander in the silent Void.
Always repenting of wrongs done
Will never bring my heart to rest.
I cast my hook in a single stream;
But my joy is as though I possessed a Kingdom.
I loose my hair and go singing;
To the four frontiers men join in my refrain.
This is the purport of my song:
'My thoughts shall wander in the Silent Void.'

[1] Famous swordsman, c. 112 B.C.

73

A GENTLE WIND

By Fu Hsüan (A.D. 217-278)

A GENTLE wind fans the calm night;
A bright moon shines on the high tower.
A voice whispers, but no one answers when I call;
A shadow stirs, but no one comes when I beckon.
The kitchen-man brings in a dish of bean-leaves;
Wine is there, but I do not fill my cup.
Contentment with poverty is Fortune's best gift;
Riches and Honour are the handmaids of Disaster.
Though gold and gems by the world are sought and prized,
To me they seem no more than weeds or chaff.

WOMAN

By Fu Hsüan

How sad it is to be framed in woman's form!
Nothing on earth is held so cheap.
A boy that comes to a home
Drops to earth like a god that chooses to be born.
His bold heart braves the Four Oceans,
The wind and dust of a thousand miles.
No one is glad when a girl is born;
By *her* the family sets no store.
When she grows up, she hides in her room
Afraid to look a man in the face.
No one cries when she leaves her home—
Sudden as clouds when the rain stops.
She bows her head and composes her face,
Her teeth are pressed on her red lips.
She bows and kneels countless times,
She must humble herself even to the servants.
While his love lasts he is distant as the stars;
She is a sun-flower, looking up to the sun.
Soon their love will be severed more than water from
        fire;
A hundred evils will be heaped upon her.
Her face will follow the year's changes;
Her lord will find new pleasures.
They that were once like substance and shadow

74

Are now as far as Hu and Ch'in.[1]
Yes, Hu and Ch'in shall sooner meet
Than they, whose parting is like Shên and Ch'ên.[2]

SATIRE ON PAYING CALLS IN AUGUST

By Ch'êng Hsiao (c. A.D. 220-264)

WHEN I was young, throughout the hot season
There were no carriages driving about the roads.
People shut their doors and lay down in the cool;
Or if they went out, it was not to pay calls.
Nowadays—ill-bred, ignorant fellows,
When they feel the heat, make for a friend's house.
The unfortunate host when he hears someone coming
Scowls and frowns, but can think of no escape.
'There's nothing for it but to rise and go to the door,'
And in his comfortable seat he groans and sighs.
The conversation does not end quickly;
Prattling and babbling, what a lot he says!
Only when one is almost dead with fatigue
He asks at last if one isn't finding him tiring.
(One's arm is almost in half with continual fanning;
The sweat is pouring down one's neck in streams).
Do not say that this is a small matter;
I consider the practice a blot on our social life.
I therefore caution all wise men
That August visitors should not be admitted.

HOT CAKE

Part of a Poem

By Shu Hsi (c. A.D. 265-306)

WINTER has come; fierce is the cold;
In the sharp morning air new-risen we meet.
Rheum freezes in the nose;
Frost hangs about the chin.
For hollow bellies, for chattering teeth and shivering knees

[1] The land of the barbarians and China.
[2] Hesperus and Lucifer.

What better than hot cake?
Soft as the down of spring,
Whiter than autumn floss!
Dense and swift the steam
Rises, swells and spreads.
Fragrance flies through the air,
Is scattered far and wide,
Steals down along the winds and wets
The covetous mouth of passer-by.
Servants and grooms
Throw sidelong glances, munch the empty air.
They lick their lips who serve;
While lines of envious lackeys by the wall
Stand dryly swallowing.

THE DESECRATION OF
THE HAN TOMBS

By CHANG TSAI (c. A.D. 289)

AT Pei-mang how they rise to Heaven,
Those high mounds, four or five in the fields!
What men lie buried under these tombs?
All of them were Lords of the Han world.
'Kung' and 'Wên'[1] gaze across at each other;
The Yüan mound is all grown over with weeds.
When the dynasty was falling, tumult and disorder arose.
Thieves and robbers roamed like wild beasts.
Of earth[2] they have crumbled more than one handful,
They have gone into vaults and opened the secret doors.
Jewelled scabbards lie twisted and defaced;
The stones that were set in them, thieves have carried away.
The ancestral temples are hummocks in the ground;
The walls that went round them are all levelled flat.
Over everything the tangled thorns are growing;
A herd-boy pushes through them up the path.
Down in the thorns rabbits have made their burrows;
The weeds and thistles will never be cleared away.
Over the tombs the ploughshare will be driven

[1] Names of two tombs.
[2] In the early days of the Han dynasty a man who stole one handful of earth from the Imperial Tombs was put to death.

And peasants will have their fields and orchards there.
They that were once lords of ten thousand chariots
Are now become the dust of the hills and ridges.
I think of what Yung-mên[1] said
And am sorely grieved at the thought of 'then' and 'now'.

DAY DREAMS

By Tso Ssŭ (died *c.* A.D. 306)

WHEN I was young, writing was my one sport,
And I read a prodigious quantity of books.
In prose I made *The Faults of Ch'in* my standard;
In verse I imitated *The Tale of Mr Nothing*.
But then the arrows began singing at the frontier
And a winged summons came flying from the City.
Although arms were not my profession
I had once read the war-book of Jang-chü.
I whooped aloud; my shouts rent the air;
I felt as though Eastern Wu were already annihilated.
The scholar's knife cuts best at its first use,
In day-dreams only are his glorious plans fulfilled;
By a glance to the left, I cleared the Yangtze and Hsiang,
By a glance to the right, I quelled the Tibetans and Hu.
When my task was done, I did not accept a barony,
But refusing with a bow retired to a cottage in the country.

THE SCHOLAR IN THE NARROW STREET

By Tso Ssŭ

FLAP, flap, the captive bird in the cage
Beating its wings against the four corners.
Sad and dreary, the scholar in the narrow street;
Clasping a shadow he dwells in an empty hut.
When he goes out, there is nowhere for him to go;
Thorns and brambles block his every path.

[1] Yung-mên said to Mêng Ch'ang-chün (died 279 B.C.), 'Does it not grieve you to think that a hundred years hence this terrace will be cast down?' Ch'ang-chün wept.

His plans are all discarded and come to nothing;
He is left stranded like a fish in a dry pond.
Without—he has not a single farthing of salary;
Within—there is not a peck of grain in his larder.
His relations all despise him for his lack of success;
Friends and companions grow daily more aloof.
Su Ch'in toured in triumph through the North,
Li Ssŭ rose to be Premier in the West;
With sudden splendour shone the flower of their fame,
With like swiftness it withered and decayed.
Though one drinks at a river, one cannot drink more than
    a belly-full;
Enough is good, but there is no use in satiety.
The bird in a forest can perch but on one bough,
And this should be the wise man's pattern.

THE VALLEY WIND

By Lu Yün (Fourth Century A.D.)

Living in retirement beyond the World,
Silently enjoying isolation,
I pull the rope of my door tighter
And bind firmly this cracked jar.[1]
My spirit is tuned to the Spring-season;
At the fall of the year there is autumn in my heart
Thus imitating cosmic changes
My cottage becomes a Universe.

A PEACOCK FLEW

(Third to Fifth Century A.D.)

A peacock flew, far off to the south-east;
Flew for a mile, then always dallied in its flight.
'At thirteen I knew how to weave silk,
At fourteen I learnt to make clothes.
At fifteen I could play the small lute,
At sixteen I knew the Songs and Book.
At seventeen I was made your wife;

[1] That serves as a window.

From care and sorrow my heart was never free,
For you already were a clerk in the great town
Diligent in your duties and caring for nothing else.
I was left alone in an empty bridal-room;
It was not often that we two could meet.
At cock-crow I went to the loom to weave;
Night after night I toiled and got no rest.
In three days I would finish five bits,
And yet the Great One[1] chid me for being slow.
Husband, it is not because I weave too slowly
That I find it hard to be a wife in your house.
It is not in my power to do the tasks I am set;
There is no use in staying for the sake of staying.
Go then quickly, speak to the lady my mistress
And while there is time let me go back to my home.'
The clerk her husband listened to her words;
Up to the Hall he went and 'Mother', he said,
'The signs of my birth marked me for a humble course;
Yet luck was with me when I took this girl to wife.
Our hair was plaited, we shared pillow and mat,
Swore friendship until the Yellow Springs of Death.
We have served you together two years or three,
Since the beginning only so little a while.
In nothing has the girl offended or done amiss;
What has happened to bring trouble between you?'
Then spoke the clerk's mother:
'Come, my son, such love is foolish doting;
This wife neglects all rules of behaviour,
And in all her ways follows her own whim.
Myself I have long been discontented with her;
You must not think only of what pleases you.
Our neighbour to eastward has a steadfast daughter;
She calls herself Lo-fu of the house of Ch'in.
The loveliest limbs that ever yet you saw!
Let mother get her for you to be your wife,
And as soon as may be send the other away;
Send her quickly, and do not let her bide.'
Long her son knelt down before her and pleaded:
'Bowing before you, mother, I make my plea.
If now you send her away
I will live single all the days of my life.'
And when his mother heard him

[1] The mother-in-law.

She banged the bed, flying into a great rage,
And 'Little son', she said, 'are you not afraid?
Dare you answer me in such a wife's praise?
By this you have forfeited all my love and kindness;
Do not dream that I will let you work your will.'
He did not speak, he made no cry.
Twice he bowed, and went back to his room;
He lifted up his voice to speak with his young bride,
But his breath caught and the words would not come.
'It is not *I* that would send you away,
It is my mother that has scolded and harried me.
Do you live at your father's, just for a little while,
For I must be going to take my orders in the town—
Not for long; I shall soon be coming home,
And when I am home, I will fetch you back again.
Let this put down the doubts that rise in your heart;
Turn it over in your thoughts and do not disobey me.'
The young wife spoke to the government clerk:
'Give me no more of this foolish tangled talk.
Long ago, when the year was at its spring,
I left my father and came to your grand home.
I obeyed my mistress in every task I plied;
Day and night I hurried on with my tasks
In solitude, caught in endless toil.
Never in word or deed was I at fault;
In tender service I waited on Madam's needs,
Yet even so she sought to send me away.
It is no use to talk of coming back.
These things are mine: a broidered waist-jacket,
Lovely and rare, shining with a light of its own;
A canopy of red gauze
With scented bags hanging at the four corners,
And shuttered boxes, sixty, seventy,
With grey marbles strung on green threads—
So many boxes, and none is like the last;
And in the boxes, so many kinds of things!
If I am vile, my things must also be scorned.
They will not be worth keeping for the after-one;[1]
Yet I leave them here; they may come in handy as
    presents.
From now onward we shall not meet again.
Once in a while let me have your news,

[1] Her successor.

And let us never, never forget one another.'

A cock crowed; outside it was growing light.
The young wife rose and tidied herself.
She puts about her a broidered, lined gown,
Takes what she needs, four or five things,
And now on her feet she slips her silk shoes;
In her hair are shining combs of tortoise-shell.
Her waist is supple as the flow of rustling silk;
At her ear she dangles a bright crescent moon.
White her fingers as the slender onion stem;
She seems in her mouth to hold cinnabar and pearls.
Slender, slender she treads with small steps,
More fine, more lovely than any lady in the world.
She goes to the Hall, low she bows her head;
But the stubborn mother's anger did not cease.
'When I was a girl', the young wife said,
'I was brought up far from any town,
A wild thing, never schooled or taught,
And needs must shame a great man's house.
From you I have taken much money and silk,
Yet was not fit to do the tasks that you set.
Today I am going back to my father's home;
I am sorry to leave you burdened by household cares.'
From her little sister[1] it was worse work to part;
Her tears fell like a string of small pearls:
'When new-wed I first came to your home,
You had just learnt to lean on the bed and walk.
Today, when I am driven away,
Little sister, you have grown as tall as me.
Work for Madam, cherish her with all your heart,
Strive to serve and help her as best you may.
Those seventh-days and last days but one[2]
Do not forget what nice romps we had!'
She left the gate, mounted her coach and went;
Of tears she dropt many hundred rows.
The clerk with his horse was riding on before;
The young wife rode in her carriage behind.
A pattering of hoofs, a thundering of wheels—
And they met each other at the mouth of the great road.

[1] -in-law.
[2] Holidays.

He left his horse and sat beside her in the coach,
He bowed his head and into her ear he spoke:
'I swear an oath that I will not give you up
If for a little while you go back to your home.
I for a little must go back to the town;
It will not be long before I am here again.
I swear by Heaven that I will not abandon you.'
'Dear husband', the young wife cried,
'Of your fond love I have not any doubt,
And since you have said you still accept me as your wife
It will not be long, I hope, before you are back.
You now must be like the great rock;
And I will be like the reed that grows by the stream.
The reed by the stream that bends but does not break;
The great rock, too mighty to move from its place.
I have a brother, my own father's son,
Whose nature and deeds are wild as a summer storm.
I fear he will not let me have my way,
And the thought of this fills my heart with dread.'
They raise their heads, bidding long farewell,
Her heart and his equally loath to part.

She enters the gate, she mounts her father's Hall,
Languidly moves with no greeting in her face.
'Child', cries her mother, and loud she claps her hands,
'We little thought to see you home so soon.
For at thirteen I taught you to weave silk,
At fourteen you could cut clothes.
At fifteen you played on the small lute,
At sixteen you knew the customs and rites.
At seventeen I sent you to be a bride
And fully thought that nothing had gone amiss.
What is your fault, what wrong have you done
That uninvited you now come back to your home?'
Then Lan-chih, ashamed before her mother,
'Oh nothing, nothing, mother, have I done amiss;'
And a deep pity tore the mother's heart.

She had been at home ten days or more
When the local magistrate sends a go-between,
Saying: 'My master has a third son,
For grace and beauty none like him in the world;
He is eighteen or nineteen years old,

A lovely boy, gifted and of ready speech.'
Then said the mother to her daughter,
'Daughter, this offer cannot be refused.'
But the daughter weeping answered,
'When I left my husband's house,
He looked kindly upon me and an oath he swore
That come what might he would not abandon me.
And today, false and wicked should I be,
Were I untrue to this our great love.
It would surely be better to break off the parley;
There is no hurry; we can answer them later on.'
Then said her mother to that go-between:
'In our humble house there is indeed a daughter,
Was once married, but came back to us again.
If she was not fit to be a clerk's wife
How can she suit a magistrate's noble son?
Pray go further and seek a better match;
At the present moment we cannot give our consent.'
Not many days had the messenger been gone
When a deputy-prefect[1] came on like quest:
'They tell me that here is a lady called Lan-chih
Whose father's fathers long served the State.
My master would have you know that his fifth son
Is handsome, clever, and has not yet a wife.
His own deputy he sends as go-between
And his deputy-assistant to carry you his words.'
The assistant told them: 'In the Lord Prefect's house
Has grown up this fine young gentleman
Who now wishes to be bound with the Great Bond,
And therefore sends us with a message to your noble
        gate.'
The girl's mother sent word to the messengers:
'This daughter of mine is already bound by a vow;
I cannot venture to speak of such a match.'
When news of this reached the brother's ear
His heart within him was much angered and vexed.
He raised his voice and thus to his sister he said:
'The plan you follow is not well considered.
Your former husband was only a Prefect's clerk;
Now you have the chance to marry a young lord!
Wide as earth from sky is the space between;

[1] As messenger from the Prefect, who was much grander than a district
magistrate.

Here is a splendour that shall brighten all your days.
But if you will not be married to this fine lord,
What refuge have you, whither else shall you turn?'
Then Lan-chih raised her hand and answered:
'Brother, there is good sense in what you say.
I left my home to serve another man,
But in mid-road[1] returned to my brother's house,
And in his hands must all my fortunes rest;
I must not ask to follow my own desire.
Though to the clerk I am bound, yet now, I think,
To eternity we shall not meet again.
Let us now accept the offer of this match
And say that the wedding may take place at once.'
The messengers left their couch, their faces beaming,
With a bland 'yes, yes' and 'so, so'.
They went to their quarters and to the Prefect they
        spoke:
'We, your servants, have fulfilled your high command;
The words we have uttered were not without effect.'
When the Lord Prefect was told of all that had passed,
His heart was filled with great mirth and joy;
He read the Calendar, he opened the sacred book.
He found it written that in this very month
The Six Points were in fortunate harmony,
The Good Omen fell in the thirtieth day;
And now already the twenty-seventh was come.
'Go, my servants, and make this wedding for me.'
With urgent message they speed the marriage gear;
Hither and thither they whirl like clouds in the sky.
A green-sparrow[2] and white-swan boat;
At its four corners a dragon-child flag
Delicately curls in the wind; a golden coach
With jade-set wheels. And dappled courses prance
With tasselled manes and saddles fretted with gold.
The wedding gift, three million cash
Pierced in the middle and strung with green thread.
Of coloured stuffs three hundred bits,
And rare fish from the markets of Chiao and Kuang.
The bridegroom's friends, four or five hundred
In great array go up to the Prefect's gate.

[1] In the mid-road of marriage.
[2] Grosbeak.

Then said the mother:
'Daughter dear, this moment a letter has come,
Saying tomorrow my Lord will fetch you away.
How comes it, girl, that you are not making your dress?
Don't leave it so late that the wedding cannot start!'
She did not answer, she did not make a sound;
With her handkerchief she covered her face and wept,
Her tears flowed like water poured from a jar.
She shifts her stool that is bright with crystal beads
And close to the front window she sets it down.
With her left hand she wields ruler and knife;
In her right hand she holds the silk gauze.
In the morning she finishes her lined, broidered gown;
By evening she has finished her thin gauze robe.
The day was over, and she in the gathering gloom
With sorrowful heart walked sobbing to the gate.
When the clerk her husband heard of what had passed
He asked for leave to return for a little while.
He had still to ride two leagues or three
When his horse neighed, raising a doleful moan.
The young wife knew the horse's neigh;
She slipped on her shoes and set out to meet him.
Woefully they looked on each other from afar,
When each saw it was his dear one that had come.
She raised her hand, she struck the horse's saddle,
Wailing and sobbing as though her heart would break.
'Since you left me——' she said,
'Things happen to one that cannot be foreseen——
It is true that I have not done as I wished to do;
But I do not think that you fully understand.
Remember that I have an own father and mother
Who with my brother forced me to do this,
Made me give myself over to another man.
How could I hope that you would ever come again?'
Then said her husband the clerk to his young wife:
'Well done!' he cried, 'well done to have climbed so high!
The great rock that is so firm and square
Was strong enough to last a thousand years.
The river reed that once was thought so tough
Was a frail thing that broke between dawn and dusk.
From glory to glory will my fine lady stride,
While I go down to the Yellow Springs alone.'
Then answered the young wife and to the clerk she said:

85

'What do you mean, why do you speak to me so?
It was the same with both; each of us was forced;
You were, and so was I too.
In the land of death you shall not be alone;
Do not fail me in what to-day you have said.'
They held hands, they parted and went their ways,
He to his house and she back to hers.
That live men can make a death-parting
Is sorrowful more than words can tell;
To know they are leaving the world and all it holds,
Doing a thing that can never be undone!

When the young clerk had got back to his home
He went to the Hall and bowing to his mother he said:
'Mother, today the great wind is cold.
A cold wind shakes the bushes and trees.
A cruel frost has stiffened the orchids in the court.
Mother, mother, to-day I go to darkness
Leaving you to stay here alone.
For my mind is set on a very sad plan;
Let your grievance against me stop when I am dead.
May your life endure like a rock of the Southern Hills,
Your back be straight and your limbs ever strong!'
When the young clerk's mother heard this
Bitter tears at each word flowed.
'O woe, will you that are of good house,
Whose father's fathers were ministers at Court
Die for a woman? Little sense do you show
Of which things matter! Listen now to my plan.
Our eastern neighbour has good girl,
Dainty and pretty, the fairest in the town.
Let Mother get her to be your wife;
I'll be quick about it; you shall have her between dawn
        and dusk.'
The clerk bowed twice, and turned to go;
Deep he sighed in the empty bridal room,
He was thinking of his plan and therefore sighing stood.
He turned his head, he moved towards the door,
Drawn by the grief that surged in his boiling breast.

That day, while horses whinnied and oxen lowed,[1]

___

[1] A bad omen.

The bride went in to her tabernacle green.
Swiftly the day closed and the dusk grew black;
There was not a sound; the second watch had begun.
'With the day that has ended my life also ends,
My soul shall go and only my body stay.'
She lifts her skirt, she takes off her silk shoes,
She rises up and walks into the blue lake.
When the young clerk heard what had happened
And knew in his heart that they had parted for ever,
He hovered a while under the courtyard tree,
Then hanged himself from the south-east bough.

The two families buried them in the same grave,
Buried them together on the side of the Hua Shan.
To east and west they planted cypress and pine,
To left and right they sowed the *wu-t'ung*.
The trees prospered; they roofed the tomb with shade,
Bough with bough, leaf with leaf entwined;
And on the boughs are two flying birds
Who name themselves Birds of True Love.
They lift their heads and face to face they sing
Every night till the fifth watch is done.
The passing traveller stays his foot to hear,
The widowed wife rises and walks her room.

This tale is a warning for the men of the afterworld;
May they learn its moral and hold it safe in their hearts.

POEMS BY T'AO CH'IEN

(A.D. 372-427)

(I)

SHADY, shady the wood in front of the Hall;
At midsummer full of calm shadows.
The south wind follows summer's train;
With its eddying puffs it blows open my coat.
I am free from ties and can live a life of retirement.
When I rise from sleep, I play with books and lute.
The lettuce in the garden still grows moist;
Of last year's grain there is always plenty left.
Self-support should maintain its strict limits;

87

More than enough is not what I want.
I grind millet and make good wine;
When the wine is heated, I pour it out for myself.
My little children are playing at my side,
Learning to talk, they babble unformed sounds.
These things have made me happy again
And I forget my lost cap of office.
Distant, distant I gaze at the white clouds;
With a deep yearning I think of the Sages of Antiquity.

(2)

IN the quiet of the morning I heard a knock at my door;
I threw on my clothes and opened it myself.
I asked who it was who had come so early to see me;
He said he was a peasant, coming with good intent.

He brought with him a full flagon of wine,
Believing my household had fallen on evil days.
'You live in rags under a thatched roof
And seem to have no desire for a better lot.
The rest of mankind have all the same ambitions;
You, too, must learn to wallow in their mire.'
'Old man, I am impressed by what you say,
But my soul is not fashioned like other men's.
To drive in their rut I might perhaps learn;
To be untrue to myself could only lead to muddle.
Let us drink and enjoy together the wine you have
        brought;
For my course is set and cannot now be altered.'

(3)

A LONG time ago
I went on a journey,
Right to the corner
Of the Eastern Ocean.
The road there
Was long and winding,
And stormy waves
Barred my path.
What made me

88

Go this way?
Hunger drove me
Into the World.
I tried hard
To fill my belly,
And even a little
Seemed a lot.
But this was clearly
A bad bargain,
So I went home
And lived in idleness.

(4)

SUBSTANCE, SHADOW, AND SPIRIT

High and low, wise and simple, all busily hoard up the moments of life. How greatly they err! Therefore I have to the uttermost exposed the bitterness both of Substance and Shadow, and have made Spirit show how, by following Nature, we may dissolve this bitterness.

Substance speaks to Shadow:

HEAVEN and Earth exist for ever;
Mountains and rivers never change.
But herbs and trees in perpetual rotation
Are renovated and withered by the dews and frosts;
And Man the wise, Man the divine—
Shall he alone escape this law?
Fortuitously appearing for a moment in the World
He suddenly departs, never to return.
Who will notice there is one person less?
His friends and relations will not give him a thought.
Only when they chance on the things he used
Day in day out, do their spirits sink for a while.
Me no magical arts can save;
Of that I am certain and cannot ever doubt.
I beg you listen to this advice—
When you get wine, be sure to drink it.

Shadow replies:

There is no way to preserve life;
Drugs of Immortality are instruments of folly.

89

I would gladly wander in Paradise,
But it is far away and there is no road.
Since the day that I was joined to you
We have shared all our joys and pains.
While you rested in the shade, I left you a while;
But till the end we shall be together.
Our joint existence is impermanent;
Sadly together we shall slip away.
That when the body decays Fame should also go
Is a thought unendurable, burning the heart.
Let us strive and labour while yet we may
To do some deed that men will praise.
Wine may in truth dispel our sorrow,
But how compare it with lasting Fame?

Spirit expounds:

God can only set in motion;
He cannot control the things he has made.
Man, the second of the Three Orders,
Owes his precedence to Me.
Though I am different from you,
We were born involved in one another;
Nor by any means can we escape
The intimate sharing of good and ill.
The Three Emperors were saintly men,
Yet to-day—where are they?
P'êng[1] lived to a great age,
Yet he went at last, when he longed to stay.
And late or soon, all go;
Wise and simple have no reprieve.
Wine may bring forgetfulness,
But does it not hasten old-age?
If you set your heart on noble deeds,
How do you know that any will praise you?
By all this thinking you do Me injury;
You had better go where Fate leads—
Drift on the Stream of Infinite Flux,
Without joy, without fear;
When you must go—then go,
And make as little fuss as you can.

The Chinese Methuselah.

(5)

CHILL and harsh the year draws to its close;
In my hempen dress I seek sunlight on the porch.
In the southern orchard all the leaves are gone;
In the north garden rotting boughs lie heaped.
I empty my cup and drink it down to the dregs;
I look towards the kitchen, but no smoke rises.
Poems and books lie piled beside my chair;
But the light is going and I shall not have time to
    read them.
My life here is not like the Agony in Ch'ên,[1]
But often I have to bear bitter reproaches.
Let me then remember, to calm my heart's distress,
That the Sages of old were often in like case.

(6)

BLAMING SONS

(An apology for his own drunkenness, A.D. 406)

WHITE hairs cover my temples,
I am wrinkled and gnarled beyond repair,
And though I have got five sons,
They all hate paper and brush.
A-shu is eighteen:
For laziness there is none like him.
A-hsüan does his best,
But really loathes the Fine Arts.
Yung and Tuan are thirteen,
But do not know 'six' from 'seven'.
T'ung-tzu in his ninth year
Is only concerned with things to eat.
If Heaven treats me like this,
What can I do but fill my cup?

(7)

I BUILT my hut in a zone of human habitation,
Yet near me there sounds no noise of horse or coach.
Would you know how that is possible?
A heart that is distant creates a wilderness round it.

Confucius was maltreated in Ch'ên.

91

I pluck chrysanthemums under the eastern hedge,
Then gaze long at the distant hills.
The mountain air is fresh at the dusk of day;
The flying birds two by two return.
In these things there lies a deep meaning;
Yet when we would express it, words suddenly fail us.

(8)

MOVING HOUSE

MY old desire to live in the Southern Village
Was not because I had taken a fancy to the house.
But I heard it was a place of simple-minded men
With whom it were a joy to spend the mornings and
    evenings.
Many years I had longed to settle here;
Now at last I have managed to move house.
I do not mind if my cottage is rather small
So long as there's room enough for bed and mat.
Often and often the neighbours come to see me
And with brave words discuss the things of old.
Rare writings we read together and praise;
Doubtful meanings we examine together and settle.

(9)

RETURNING TO THE FIELDS

WHEN I was young, I was out of tune with the herd;
My only love was for the hills and mountains.
Unwitting I fell into the Web of the World's dust
And was not free until my thirtieth year.
The migrant bird longs for the old wood;
The fish in the tank thinks of its native pool.
I had rescued from wildness a patch of the Southern Moor
And, still rustic, I returned to field and garden.
My ground covers no more than ten acres;
My thatched cottage has eight or nine rooms.
Elms and willows cluster by the eaves;
Peach trees and plum trees grow before the Hall.
Hazy, hazy the distant hamlets of men;
Steady the smoke that hangs over cottage roofs.

A dog barks somewhere in the deep lanes,
A cock crows at the top of the mulberry tree.
At gate and courtyard—no murmur of the World's dust;
In the empty rooms—leisure and deep stillness.
Long I lived checked by the bars of a cage;
Now I have turned again to Nature and Freedom.

(10)

READING THE BOOK OF HILLS AND SEAS

In the month of June the grass grows high
And round my cottage thick-leaved branches sway.
There is not a bird but delights in the place where it rests;
And I too—love my thatched cottage.
I have done my ploughing;
I have sown my seed.
Again I have time to sit and read my books.
In the narrow lane there are no deep ruts;
Often my friends' carriages turn back.
In high spirits I pour out my spring wine
And pluck the lettuce growing in my garden.
A gentle rain comes stealing up from the east
And a sweet wind bears it company.
My thoughts float idly over the story of the king of Chou,
My eyes wander over the pictures of Hills and Seas.
At a single glance I survey the whole Universe.
He will never be happy, whom such pleasures fail to please!

(11)

FLOOD

The lingering clouds, rolling, rolling,
And the settled rain, dripping, dripping,
In the Eight Directions—the same dusk.
The level lands—one great river.
Wine I have, wine I have;
Idly I drink at the eastern window.
Longingly—I think of my friends,
But neither boat nor carriage comes.

93

NEW CORN

SWIFTLY the years, beyond recall.
Solemn the stillness of this fair morning.
I will clothe myself in spring-clothing
And visit the slopes of the Eastern Hill.
By the mountain-stream a mist hovers,
Hovers a moment, then scatters.
There comes a wind blowing from the south
That brushes the fields of new corn.

SAILING HOMEWARD

By CHAN FANG-SHÊNG

(*c.* A.D. 400)

CLIFFS that rise a thousand feet
Without a break,
Lake that stretches a hundred miles
Without a wave,
Sands that are white through all the year
Without a stain,
Pine-tree woods, winter and summer
Ever-green,
Streams that for ever flow and flow
Without a pause,
Trees that for twenty thousand years
Your vows have kept,
You have suddenly healed the pain of a traveller's
        heart,
And moved his brush to write a new song.

FOLK-SONGS

(Fourth or Fifth Century A.D.)

I HAVE brought my pillow and am lying at the northern
        window,
So come to me and play with me a while.
With so much roughness and so little play
How long do you think our love can last?

I will gather up my skirt, but not put on my belt;
I will trim my eyebrows and stand at the front window.
My tiresome petticoat keeps on flapping about;
If it opens a little I shall say it was the spring wind.

I am steadfast as the star of the Northern Pole;
In a thousand years it never shifts from its place.
You have ways that are like the bright sun;
In the morning, east; in the evening again west.

When dusk gathered you came in over the hedge;
But when dawn was near you sallied out at the gate.
Alas that my dear one should care only for himself;
What happens to me he does not care at all.

At the fifth watch I rose and opened the door
Just in time to see my love go by.
'Where do you come from, where have you spent the night,
Dear love, that your clothes are covered with frost and dew?'

I heard my love was going to Yang-chow
And went with him as far as Ch'u Hill.
For a moment, when you held me fast in your outstretched
    arms
I thought the river stood still and did not flow.

THE LITTLE LADY OF CH'ING-CH'I

A Children's Song

> HER door opened on the white water
> Close by the side of the timber bridge;
> That's where the little lady lived
> All alone without a lover.

PLUCKING THE RUSHES

A boy and girl are sent to gather rushes for thatching.
    Anon. (Fourth or Fifth Century)

> GREEN rushes with red shoots,
> Long leaves bending to the wind—
> You and I in the same boat

Plucking rushes at the Five Lakes.
We started at dawn from the orchid-island;
We rested under the elms till noon.
You and I plucking rushes
Had not plucked a handful when night came!

BALLAD OF THE WESTERN ISLAND
IN THE NORTH COUNTRY

'SEEING the plum-tree I thought of the Western Island
And I plucked a branch to send to the North Country.
I put on my dress of apricot-yellow silk
And bound up my hair black as the crow's wing.
But which is the road that leads to the Western Island?
I'll ask the man at the ferry by the Bridge of Boats.
But the sun is sinking and the orioles flying home;
And the wind is blowing and sighing in the walnut-tree.
I'll stand under the tree just beside the gate;
I'll stand by the door and show off my enamelled hair-pins.'
She's opened the gate, but her lover has not come;
She's gone out at the gate to pluck red lotus.
As she plucks the lotus on the southern dyke in autumn,
The lotus flowers stand higher than a man's head.
She bends down—and plays with the lotus seeds,
The lotus seeds are green like the lake-water.
She gathers the flowers and puts them into her gown—
The lotus-bud that is red all through.
She thinks of her lover, her lover that does not come;
She looks up and sees the wild geese flying—
The Western Island is full of wild geese.
To look for her lover she climbs the Blue Tower.
The tower is high: she looks, but cannot see;
All day she leans on the balcony rails.
The rail is twisted into a twelve-fold pattern.
She lets fall her hand white like the colour of jade.
She rolls up the awning, she sees the wide sky,
And the sea-water waving its vacant blue.
'The sea shall carry my dreams far away,
So that you shall be sorry at last for my sorrow.
If the South wind only knew my thoughts
It would blow my dreams till they got to the Western Island.'

SONG OF THE MEN OF CHIN-LING

(Marching back into the Capital)
By Hsieh T'iao (A.D. 464-499)

Chiang-nan[1] is a glorious and beautiful land
And Chin-ling[2] an exalted and kingly province!
The green canals of the city twist and coil
And its high towers stretch up and up.
Flying gables lean over the bridle-road;
Drooping willows cover the Royal Aqueduct.
Shrill flutes sing by the coach's awning,
And reiterated drums bang near its painted wheels.
The names of the deserving shall be presented at the
 Cloud Terrace;
For those who have done valiantly rich reward awaits.

DREAMING OF A DEAD LADY

By Shên Yo (A.D. 441-513)

'I heard at nights your long sighs
And knew that you were thinking of me.'
As she spoke, the doors of Heaven opened;
Our souls conversed and I saw her face.

She set me a pillow to rest on;
She brought me meat and drink.
I stood beside her where she lay,
But suddenly woke and she was not there.
And none knew how my soul was torn,
How the tears fell surging over my breast.

PEOPLE HIDE THEIR LOVE

By Wu-ti, Emperor of the Liang Dynasty (A.D. 464-549)

Who says that it's by my desire,
This separation, this living so far from you?
My dress still smells of the perfume that you wore;
My hand still holds the letter that you sent.

[1] 'South of the River.'   [2] South-west of Nanking.

Round my waist I wear a double sash;
I dream that it binds us both with a same-heart knot.
Did you know that people hide their love,
Like a flower that seems too precious to be picked?

SUMMER SONG

By WU TI

AT the time when blossoms fall from the cherry-tree,
On a day when orioles flitted from bough to bough,
You said you must stop, because your horse was tired;
I said I must go, because my silkworms were hungry.

LO-YANG

By the EMPEROR CHIEN WÊN-TI (A.D. 503-551)

A BEAUTIFUL place is the town of Lo-yang;
The big streets are full of spring light.
The lads go driving out with lutes in their hands;
The mulberry girls go out to the fields with their baskets.
Golden saddles glint at the horses' flanks,
Gauze sleeves brush the green boughs.
Racing dawn, the carriages come home—
And the girls with their high baskets full of fruit.

WINTER NIGHT

By CHIEN WÊN-TI

MY bed is so empty that I keep on waking up;
As the cold increases, the night-wind begins to blow.
It rustles the curtains, making a noise like the sea.
Oh that those were waves which could carry me back to you!

THE WATERS OF LUNG-T'OU

(The North-West Frontier)
By HSÜ LING (A.D. 507-583)

THE road that I came by mounts eight thousand feet;
The river that I crossed hangs a hundred fathoms.
The brambles so thick that in summer one cannot pass;
The snow so high that in winter one cannot climb!
With branches that interlace Lung Valley is dark;
Against cliffs that tower one's voice beats and echoes.
I turn my head, and it seems only a dream
That I ever lived in the streets of Hsien-yang.

TELEG SONG

(Sixth Century A.D.)

TELEG River
Lies under the Dark Mountains,
Where the sky is like the sides of a tent
Stretched down over the Great Steppe.
The sky is grey, grey
And the steppe wide, wide.
Over grass that the wind has battered low
Sheep and oxen roam.

THE BALLAD OF MULAN

(Written in northern China during the domination of the Wei
Tartars, Sixth Century A.D.)

CLICK, click, for ever click, click;
Mulan sits at the door and weaves.
Listen, and you will not hear the shuttle's sound,
But only hear a girl's sobs and sighs.
'Oh, tell me, lady, are you thinking of your love,
Oh tell me, lady, are you longing for your dear?'
'Oh no, oh no, I am not thinking of my love,
Oh no, oh no, I am not longing for my dear.
But last night I read the battle-roll;
The Khan has ordered a great levy of men.
The battle-roll was written in twelve books,

99

And in each book stood my father's name.
My father's sons are not grown men,
And of all my brothers, none is older than me.
Oh let me to the market to buy saddle and horse,
And ride with the soldiers to take my father's place.'
In the eastern market she's bought a gallant horse,
In the western market she's bought saddle and cloth.
In the southern market she's bought snaffle and reins,
In the northern market she's bought a tall whip.
In the morning she stole from her father's and mother's house;
At night she was camping by the Yellow River's side.
She could not hear her father and mother calling to her by
    her name,
But only the voice of the Yellow River as its waters swirled
    through the night.
At dawn they left the River and went on their way;
At dusk they came to the Black Water's side.
She could not hear her father and mother calling to her by her
    name,
She could only hear the muffled voices of foreign horsemen
    riding on the hills of Yen.
A thousand leagues she tramped on the errands of war,
Frontiers and hills she crossed like a bird in flight.
Through the northern air echoed the watchman's tap;
The wintry light gleamed on coats of mail.
The captain had fought a hundred fights, and died;
The warriors in ten years had won their rest.
They went home, they saw the Emperor's face;
The Son of Heaven was seated in the Hall of Light.
The deeds of the brave were recorded in twelve books;
In prizes he gave a hundred thousand cash.
Then spoke the Khan and asked her what she would take.
'Oh, Mulan asks not to be made
    A Counsellor at the Khan's court;
I only beg for a camel that can march
    A thousand leagues a day,
      To take me back to my home.'

When her father and mother heard that she had come,
They went out to the wall and led her back to the house.
When her little sister heard that she had come,
She went to the door and rouged her face afresh.
When her little brother heard that his sister had come,

He sharpened his knife and darted like a flash
Towards the pigs and sheep.
She opened the gate that leads to the eastern tower,
She sat on her bed that stood in the western tower.
She cast aside her heavy soldier's cloak,
And wore again her old-time dress.
She stood at the window and bound her cloudy hair;
She went to the mirror and fastened her yellow combs.
She left the house and met her messmates in the road;
Her messmates were startled out of their wits.
They had marched with her for twelve years of war
And never known that Mulan was a girl.
For the male hare sits with its legs tucked in,
And the female hare in known for her bleary eye;
But set them both scampering side by side,
And who so wise could tell you 'This is he?'

FLOWERS AND MOONLIGHT ON THE SPRING RIVER

By YANG-TI, Emperor of the Sui Dynasty from 605 till 617.

THE evening river is level and motionless—
The spring colours just open to their full.
Suddenly a wave carries the moon away
And the tidal water comes with its freight of stars.

COCK-CROW SONG
Anon. (Sixth Century A.D. ?)

IN the eastern quarter dawn breaks, the stars flicker pale;
The Morning Cock[1] from Ju-nan mounts his stand and calls.
The song is over, the clock[2] run down, the mats and screens
    are set;
The moon grows dim and the stars are few; morning has come
    to the world.

[1] Fowls were not kept in the Palace, so a watchman woke the Court by
singing this song. These watchmen came from Ju-nan in Honan.
[2] A water-clock.

At a thousand gates and ten thousand doors the fish-shaped[1]
    bolts are drawn;
Round the Palace and up over the walls crows and magpies
    are flying.

TELL ME NOW

By WANG CHI (A.D. 584-644)

'TELL me now, what should a man want
But to sit alone, sipping his cup of wine?'
I should like to have visitors come and discuss philosophy
And not to have the tax-collector coming to collect taxes;
My three sons married into good families
And my five daughters wedded to steady husbands.
Then I could jog through a happy five-score years
And, at the end, need no Paradise.

BUSINESS MEN

By CH'ÊN TZŬ-ANG (A.D. 656-698)

BUSINESS men boast of their skill and cunning
But in philosophy they are like little children.
Bragging to each other of successful depredations
They neglect to consider the ultimate fate of the body.
What should they know of the Master of Dark Truth
Who saw the wide world in a jade cup,
By illumined conception got clear of Heaven and Earth,
On the chariot of Mutation entered the Gate of Immutability?

IN THE MOUNTAINS ON A
SUMMER DAY

By LI PO (A.D. 701-762)

GENTLY I stir a white feather fan,
With open shirt sitting in a green wood.
I take off my cap and hang it on a jutting stone;
A wind from the pine-tree trickles on my bare head.

[1] The fish, which never sleeps, is a symbol of watchfulness.

SELF-ABANDONMENT

By Li Po

I sat drinking and did not notice the dusk,
Till falling petals filled the folds of my dress.
Drunken I rose and walked to the moonlit stream;
The birds were gone, and men also few.

TO TAN-CH'IU

By Li Po

My friend is lodging high in the Eastern Range,
Dearly loving the beauty of valleys and hills.
At green Spring he lies in the empty woods,
And is still asleep when the sun shines on high.
A pine-tree wind dusts his sleeves and coat;
A pebbly stream cleans his heart and ears.
I envy you, who far from strife and talk
Are high-propped on a pillow of blue cloud.

CLEARING AT DAWN

By Li Po

The fields are chill, the sparse rain has stopped;
The colours of Spring teem on every side.
With leaping fish the blue pond is full;
With singing thrushes the green boughs droop.
The flowers of the field have dabbled their powdered cheeks;
The mountain grasses are bent level at the waist.
By the bamboo stream the last fragment of cloud
Blown by the wind slowly scatters away.

STONE FISH LAKE

By Yüan Chieh (A.D. 719-772)

I loved you dearly, Stone Fish Lake,
With your rock-island shaped like a swimming fish!
On the fish's back is the Wine-cup Hollow
And round the fish—the flowing waters of the Lake.
The boys on the shore sent little wooden ships,

Each made to carry a single cup of wine.
The island-drinkers emptied the liquor boats
And set their sails and sent them back for more.
On the shores of the Lake were jutting slabs of rock
And under the rocks there flowed an icy stream.
Heated with wine, to rinse our mouths and hands
In those cold waters was a joy beyond compare!

Of gold and jewels I have not any need;
For Caps and Coaches I do not care at all.
But I wish I could sit on the rocky banks of the Lake
For ever and ever staring at the Stone Fish.

CIVILIZATION

By Yüan Chieh

To the south-east—three thousand leagues—
The Yüan and Hsiang form into a mighty lake.
Above the lake are deep mountain valleys,
And men dwelling whose hearts are without guile.
Gay like children, they swarm to the tops of the trees;
And run to the water to catch bream and trout.
Their pleasures are the same as those of beasts and birds;
They put no restraint either on body or mind.
Far I have wandered throughout the Nine Lands;
Wherever I went such manners had disappeared.
I find myself standing and wondering, perplexed,
Whether Saints and Sages have really done us good.

HEARING THAT HIS FRIEND WAS COMING BACK FROM THE WAR

By Wang Chien (c. A.D. 756-835)

In old days those who went to fight
In three years had one year's leave.
But in *this* war the soldiers are never changed;
They must go on fighting till they die on the battlefield.
I thought of you, so weak and indolent,
Hopelessly trying to learn to march and drill.
That a young man should ever come home again
Seemed about as likely as that the sky should fall.

Since I got the news that you were coming back,
Twice I have mounted to the high wall of your home.
I found your brother mending your horse's stall;
I found your mother sewing your new clothes.
I am half afraid; perhaps it is not true;
Yet I never weary of watching for you on the road.
Each day I go out at the City Gate
With a flask of wine, lest you should come thirsty.
Oh that I could shrink the surface of the World,
So that suddenly I might find you standing at my side!

THE SOUTH

By WANG CHIEN

IN the southern land many birds sing;
Of towns and cities half are unwalled.
The country markets are thronged by wild tribes;
The mountain-villages bear river-names.
Poisonous mists rise from the damp sands;
Strange fires gleam through the night-rain.
And none passes but the lonely seeker of pearls
Year by year on his way to the South Sea.

POEMS BY HAN-SHAN

The Chinese poet Han-shan lived in the 8th and 9th centuries.
He and his brothers worked a farm that they had inherited; but
he fell out with them, parted from his wife and family, and
wandered from place to place, reading many books and looking
in vain for a patron. He finally settled as a recluse on the Cold
Mountain (Han-shan) and is always known as 'Han-shan.' This
retreat was about twenty-five miles from T'ien-t'ai, famous for
its many monasteries, both Buddhist and Taoist, which Han-
shan visited from time to time. In one poem he speaks of himself
as being over a hundred. This may be an exaggeration; but it is
certain that he lived to a great age.

In his poems the Cold Mountain is often the name of a state
of mind rather than of a locality. It is on this conception, as well
as on that of the 'hidden treasure,' the Buddha who is to be
sought not somewhere outside us, but 'at home' in the heart,
that the mysticism of the poems is based.

The poems, of which just over three hundred survive, have
no titles.

FROM my father and mother I inherited land enough

And need not envy others' orchards and fields.
Creak, creak goes the sound of my wife's loom;
Back and forth my children prattle at their play.
They clap their hands to make the flowers dance;
Then chin on palm listen to the birds' song.
Does anyone ever come to pay his respects?
Yes, there is a woodcutter who often comes this way.

I have thatched my rafters and made a peasant hut;
Horse and carriage seldom come to my gate—
Deep in the woods, where birds love to forgather,
By a broad stream, the home of many fish.
The mountain fruits child in hand I pluck;
My paddy field along with my wife I hoe.
And what have I got inside my house?
Nothing at all but one stand of books.

When I was young I weeded book in hand,
Sharing at first a home with my elder brothers.
Something happened, and they put the blame on me;
Even my own wife turned against me.
So I left the red dust of the world and wandered
Hither and thither, reading book after book
And looking for some one who would spare a drop of water
To keep alive the gudgeon in the carriage rut.

Wretched indeed is the scholar without money;
Who else knows such hunger and cold?
Having nothing to do he takes to writing poems,
He grinds them out till his thoughts refuse to work.
For a starveling's words no one has any use;
Accept the fact and cease your doleful sighs.
Even if you wrote your verses on a macaroon
And gave them to the dog, the dog would refuse to eat.

Wise men, you have forsaken me;
Foolish men, I have forsaken you.
Being not foolish and also not wise
Henceforward I shall hear from you no more.
When night falls I sing to the bright moon,
At break of dawn I dance among the white clouds.
Would you have me with closed lips and folded hands
Sit up straight, waiting for my hair to go grey?

I am sometimes asked the way to the Cold Mountain;
There is no path that goes all the way.
Even in summer the ice never melts;
Far into the morning the mists gather thick.
How, you may ask, did I manage to get here?
My heart is not like your heart.
If only your heart were like mine
You too would be living where I live now.

Long, long the way to the Cold Mountain;
Stony, stony the banks of the chill stream.
Twitter, twitter—always there are birds;
Lorn and lone—no human but oneself.
Slip, slap the wind blows in one's face;
Flake by flake the snow piles on one's clothes.
Day after day one never sees the sun;
Year after year knows no spring.

I make my way up the Cold Mountain path;
The way up seems never to end.
The valley so long and the ground so stony;
The stream so broad and the brush so tangled and thick.
The moss is slippery, rain or no rain;
The pine-trees sing even when no wind blows.
Who can bring himself to transcend the bonds of the world
And sit with me among the white clouds?

Pile on pile, the glories of hill and stream;
Sunset mists enclose flanks of blue.
Brushed by the storm my gauze cap is wet;
The dew damps my straw-plaited coat.
My feet shod with stout pilgrim-shoes,
My hand grasping my old holly staff
Looking again beyond the dusty world
What use have I for a land of empty dreams?

I went off quietly to visit a wise monk,
Where misty mountains rose in myriad piles.
The Master himself showed me my way back,
Pointing to where the moon, that round lamp, hung.

In old days, when I was very poor,
Night by night I counted another's treasures.
There came a time when I thought things over
And decided to set up in business on my own.

So I dug at home and came upon a buried treasure;
A ball of saphire—that and nothing less!
There came a crowd of blue-eyed traders from the West
Who had planned together to bid for it and take it away.
But I straightway answered those merchants, saying
'This is a jewel that no price could buy.'

Leisurely I wandered to the top of the Flowery Peak;
The day was calm and the morning sun flashed.
I looked into the clear sky on every side.
A white cloud was winging its crane's flight.

I have for dwelling the shelter of a green cliff;
For garden, a thicket that knife has never trimmed.
Over it the fresh creepers hang their coils;
Ancient rocks stand straight and tall.
The mountain fruits I leave for the monkeys to pick;
The fish of the pool vanish into the heron's beak.
Taoist writings, one volume or two,
Under the trees I read—*nam, nam.*

The season's change has ended a dismal year;
Spring has come and the colours of things are fresh.
Mountain flowers laugh into the green pools,
The trees on the rock dance in the blue mist.
Bees and butterflies pursue their own pleasure;
Birds and fishes are there for my delight.
Thrilled with feelings of endless comradeship
From dusk to dawn I could not close my eyes.

A place to prize is this Cold Mountain,
Whose white clouds for ever idle on their own,
Where the cry of monkeys spreads among the paths,
Where the tiger's roar transcends the world of men.
Walking alone I step from stone to stone,
Singing to myself I clutch at the creepers for support.
The wind in the pine-trees makes its shrill note;
The chatter of the birds mingles its harmony.

The people of the world when they see Han-shan
All regard him as not in his right mind.
His appearance, they say, is far from being attractive,
Tied up as he is in bits of tattered cloth.
'What we say, he cannot understand;

What he says, we do not say.'
You who spend all your time in coming and going,
Why not try for once coming to the Han-shan?

Ever since the time when I hid in the Cold Mountain
I have kept alive by eating the mountain fruits.
From day to day what is there to trouble me?
This my life follows a destined course.
The days and months flow ceaseless as a stream;
Our time is brief as the flash struck on a stone.
If Heaven and Earth shift, then let them shift;
I shall still be sitting happy among the rocks.

When the men of the world look for this path amid the clouds
It vanishes, with not a trace where it lay.
The high peaks have many precipices;
On the widest gulleys hardly a gleam falls.
Green walls close behind and before;
White clouds gather east and west.
Do you want to know where the cloud-path lies?
The cloud-path leads from sky to sky.

Since first I meant to explore the eastern cliff
And have not done so, countless years have passed.
Yesterday I pulled myself up by the creepers,
But half way, was baffled by storm and fog.
The cleft so narrow that my clothing got caught fast;
The moss so sticky that I could not free my shoes.
So I stopped here under this red cinnamon,
To sleep for a while on a pillow of white clouds.

Sitting alone I am sometimes overcome
By vague feelings of sadness and unrest.
Round the waist of the hill the clouds stretch and stretch;
At the mouth of the valley the winds sough and sigh.
A monkey comes; the trees bend and sway;
A bird goes into the wood with a shrill cry.
Time hastens the grey that wilts on my brow;
The year is over, and age is comfortless.

Last year when the spring birds were singing
At this time I thought about my brothers.
This year when chrysanthemums are fading
At this time the same thought comes back.
Green waters sob in a thousand streams,

Dark clouds lie flat on every side.
Till life ends, though I live a hundred years,
It will rend my heart to think of Ch'ang-an.

In the third month when the silkworms were still small
The girls had time to go and gather flowers,
Along the wall they played with the butterflies,
Down by the water they pelted the old frog.
Into gauze sleeves they poured the ripe plums;
With their gold hairpins they dug up bamboo-sprouts.
With all that glitter of outward loveliness
How can the Cold Mountain hope to compete?

Last night I dreamt that I was back in my home
And saw my wife weaving at her loom.
She stayed her shuttle as though thinking of something;
When she lifted it again it was as though she had no strength.
I called to her and she turned her head and looked;
She stared blankly, she did not know who I was.
Small wonder, for we parted years ago
When the hair on my temples was still its old colour.

I have sat here facing the Cold Mountain
Without budging for twenty-nine years.
Yesterday I went to visit friends and relations;
A good half had gone to the Springs of Death.
Life like a guttering candle wears away—
A stream whose waters forever flow and flow.
Today, with only my shadow for company,
Astonished I find two tear-drops hang.

In old days (how long ago it was!)
I remember a house that was lovelier than all the rest.
Peach and plum lined the little paths;
Orchid and iris grew by the stream below.
There walked beside it girls in satins and silks;
Within there glinted a robe of kingfisher-green.
That was how we met; I tried to call her to me,
But my tongue stuck and the words would not come.

I sit and gaze on this highest peak of all;
Wherever I look there is distance without end.
I am all alone and no one knows I am here,
A lonely moon is mirrored in the cold pool.
Down in the pool there is not really a moon;

The only moon is in the sky above.
I sing to you this one piece of song;
But in the song there is not any Zen.

Should you look for a parable of life and death
Ice and water are the true comparisons.
Water binds and turns into ice;
Ice melts and again becomes water.
Whatever has died will certainly be born,
Whatever has come to life must needs die.
Ice and water do each other no harm;
Life and death too are both good.

POEMS BY PO CHÜ-I

Life of Po Chü-i

772 Born on 20th of first month.
800 Passes his Examinations.
806 Receives a minor post at Chou-chih, near the capital.
807 Made Scholar of the Han Lin Academy.
811 Retires to Wei River, being in mourning for his mother.
812 Returns to Court.
814 Banished to Hsün-yang.
818 Removed to Chung-chou.
820 Reprieved and returns to Court.
822 Governor of Hangchow.
825 Governor of Soochow.
826 Retires owing to illness.
827 Returns to Ch'ang-an.
829 Settles permanently at Lo-yang.
831 Governor of Ho-nan, the province of which Lo-yang was capital.
833 Retires owing to illness.
839 Has paralytic stroke in tenth month.
846 Dies in the eighth month.

AFTER PASSING THE EXAMINATION

(A.D. 800)

FOR ten years I never left my books;
I went up . . . and won unmerited praise.
My high place I do not much prize;
The joy of my parents will first make me proud.

Fellow students, six or seven men,
See me off as I leave the City gate.
My covered coach is ready to drive away;
Flutes and strings blend their parting tune.
Hopes achieved dull the pains of parting;
Fumes of wine shorten the long road. . . .
Shod with wings is the horse of him who rides
On a Spring day the road that leads to home.

ESCORTING CANDIDATES TO THE EXAMINATION HALL

(A.D. 805)

At dawn I rode to escort the Doctors of Art;
In the eastern quarter the sky was still grey.
I said to myself: 'You have started far too soon,'
But horses and coaches already thronged the road.
High and low the riders' torches bobbed;
Muffled or loud, the watchman's drum beat.
Riders, when I see you trot, so pleased with yourselves
To your early levee, pity fills my heart.
When the sun rises and the hot dust flies
And the creatures of earth resume their great strife,
You, with your striving, what shall you each seek?
Profit and fame, for that is all your care.
But I, you courtiers, rise from my bed at noon
And live idly in the city of Ch'ang-an.
Spring is deep and my term of office spent;
Day by day my thoughts go back to the hills.

IN EARLY SUMMER LODGING IN A TEMPLE TO ENJOY THE MOONLIGHT

(A.D. 805)

In early summer, with two or three more
That were seeking fame in the city of Ch'ang-an,
Whose low employ gave them less business
Than ever they had since first they left their homes—
With these I wandered deep into the shrine of Tao,
For the joy we sought was promised in this place.

When we reached the gate, we sent our coaches back;
We entered the yard with only cap and stick.
Still and clear, the first weeks of May,
When trees are green and bushes soft and wet;
When the wind freshens the shadows of new leaves
And birds linger on the last boughs that bloom.
Towards evening when the sky grew clearer yet
And the South-east was still clothed in red,
To the western cloister we carried our jar of wine;
We waited for the moon before starting to drink.
Soon, how soon her golden ghost was born,
Swiftly, as though she had waited for us to come.
The beams of her light shone in every place,
On towers and halls dancing to and fro.
Till day broke we sat in her clear light
Laughing and singing, and yet never grew tired.
In Ch'ang-an, the place of profit and fame,
Such moods as this, how many men know?

BEING ON DUTY ALL NIGHT IN THE PALACE AND DREAMING OF THE HSIEN-YU TEMPLE

AT the western window I paused from writing rescripts;
The pines and bamboos were all buried in stillness.
The moon rose and a calm wind came;
Suddenly, it was like an evening in the hills.
And so, as I dozed, I dreamed of the South West
And thought I was staying at the Hsien-yu Temple.
When I woke and heard the dripping of the Palace clock
I still thought it the trickle of a mountain stream.

WATCHING THE REAPERS

(A.D. 806)

TILLERS of the earth have few idle months;
In the fifth month their toil is double-fold.
A south wind visits the fields at night;
Suddenly the ridges are covered with yellow corn.
Wives and daughters shoulder baskets of rice,

Youths and boys carry flasks of wine,
In a long train, to feed the workers in the field—
The strong reapers toiling on the southern hill,
Whose feet are burned by the hot earth they tread,
Whose backs are scorched by the flames of the shining sky
Tired they toil, caring nothing for the heat,
Grudging the shortness of the long summer day.
A poor woman with a young child at her side
Follows behind, to glean the unwanted grain.
In her right hand she holds the fallen ears,
On her left arm a broken basket hangs.
Listening to what they said as they worked together
I heard something that made me very sad:
They lost in grain-tax the whole of their own crop;
What they glean here is all they will have to eat.

And I today—in virtue of what desert
Have I never once tended field or tree?
My government-pay is three hundred 'stones';
At the year's end I have still grain in hand.
Thinking of this, secretly I grew ashamed
And all day the thought lingered in my head.

SICK LEAVE

(While Chief Clerk to the sub-prefecture of Chou-chih, near
Ch'ang-an, in A.D. 806)

PROPPED on pillows, not attending to business;
For two days I've lain behind locked doors.
I begin to think that those who hold office
Get no rest, except by falling ill!
For restful thoughts one does not need space;
The room where I lie is ten foot square.
By the western eaves, above the bamboo-twigs,
From my couch I see the White Mountain rise.
But the clouds that hover on its far-distant peak
Bring shame to a face that is buried in the World's dust.

GOING ALONE TO SPEND A NIGHT AT THE HSIEN-YU TEMPLE

(A.D. 806)

THE crane from the shore standing at the top of the steps
The moon on the pool seen at the open door;
Where these are, I made my lodging-place
And for two nights could not turn away.
I am glad I chanced on a place so lonely and still
With no companion to drag me early home.
Now that I have tasted the joy of being alone,
I will never again come with a friend at my side.

PLANTING BAMBOOS

(A.D. 806 ?)

I AM not suited for service in a country town;
At my closed door autumn grasses grow.
What could I do to ease a rustic heart ?
I planted bamboos, more than a hundred shoots.
When I see their beauty, as they grow by the stream-side,
I feel again as though I lived in the hills,
And many a time when I have not much work
Round their railing I walk till night comes.
Do not say that their roots are still weak,
Do not say that their shade is still small;
Already I feel that both in courtyard and house
Day by day a fresher air moves.
But most I love, lying near the window-side,
To hear in their branches the sound of the autumn wind.

PASSING T'IEN-MÊN STREET IN CH'ANG-AN AND SEEING A DISTANT VIEW OF CHUNG-NAN MOUNTAINS

THE snow has gone from Chung-nan; spring is almost come.
Lovely in the distance its blue colours, against the brown of
the streets.

A thousand coaches, ten thousand horsemen pass down the Nine
    Roads;
Turns his head and looks at the mountains—not one man!

TO LI CHIEN

Part of a Poem
(A.D. 810)

WORLDLY matters again draw my body;
Worldly things again seduce my heart.
Whenever for long I part from Li Chien
Gradually my thoughts grow narrow and covetous.
I remember how once I used to visit you;
I stopped my horse and tapped at the garden-gate.
Often when I came you were still lying in bed;
Your little children were sent to let me in.
And you, laughing, ran to the front-door
With coat-tails flying and cap all awry.
On the swept terrace, green patterns of moss;
On the dusted bench the shade of the creepers was cool.
To gaze at the hills we sat in the eastern lodge;
To wait for the noon we walked to the southern moor.
At your quiet gate only birds spoke;
In your distant street few drums were heard.
Opposite each other all day we talked,
And never once spoke of profit or fame.
Since we parted hands, how long has passed?
Thrice and again the full moon has shone.
For when we parted the last flowers were falling,
And today I hear new cicadas sing.
The scented year suddenly draws to its close,
Yet the sorrow of parting is still unsubdued.

THE OLD LUTE

OF cord and cassia-wood is the lute compounded;
Within it lie ancient melodies.
Ancient melodies—weak and savourless,
Not appealing to present men's taste.

Light and colour are faded from the jade stops;
Dust has covered the rose-red strings.
Decay and ruin came to it long ago,
But the sound that is left is still cold and clear.
I do not refuse to play it, if you want me to;
But even if I play, people will not listen.

.　　　.　　　.

How did it come to be neglected so?
Because of the Ch'iang flute and the zithern of Ch'in.[1]

THE PRISONER

(Written *c.* A.D. 809)

TARTARS led in chains,
Tartars led in chains!
Their ears pierced, their faces bruised—they are driven into the
　　land of Ch'in.
The Son of Heaven took pity on them and would not have them
　　slain.
He sent them away to the south-east, to the lands of Wu and
　　Yüeh.
A petty officer in a yellow coat took down their names and surnames;
They were led from the city of Ch'ang-an by relays of armed guards.
Their bodies were covered with the wounds of arrows, their bones
　　stood out from their cheeks.
They had grown so weak they could only march a single stage a
　　day.
In the morning they must satisfy hunger and thirst with neither
　　plate nor cup;
At night they must lie in their dirt and rags on beds that stank with
　　filth.
Suddenly they came to the Yangtze River and remembered the
　　waters of Chiao.[2]
With lowered hands and levelled voices they sobbed a muffled song.
Then one Tartar lifted up his voice and spoke to the other Tartars,
'Your sorrows are none at all compared with my sorrows.'
Those that were with him in the same band asked to hear his tale;
As he tried to speak the words were choked by anger.

[1] Non-classical instruments.
[2] In Turkestan.

117

He told them 'I was born and bred in the plain of Liang-chou;[1]
In the frontier wars of Ta-li[2] I fell into the Tartars' hands.
Since the days the Tartars took me alive, forty years ago,
I have had to wear a coat of skins tied with a fur belt.
Only on the first of the first month might I wear my Chinese dress.
As I put on my coat and arranged my cap, how fast the tears flowed!
I made in my heart a secret vow I would find a way home;
I hid my plan from my Tartar wife and the children she had borne
    me in the land.
I thought to myself, "It is well for me that my limbs are still strong,"
And yet, being old, in my heart I feared I should never live to return.
The Tartar chieftains shoot so well that the birds are afraid to fly;
From the risk of their arrows I escaped alive and fled swiftly home.
Hiding all day and walking all night, I crossed the Great Desert,[3]
Where clouds are dark and the moon black and the sands eddy in
    the wind.
Frightened, I sheltered at the Green Grave,[4] where the frozen
    grasses are few;
Stealthily I crossed the Yellow River, at night, on the thin ice,
Suddenly I heard Han[5] drums and the sound of soldiers coming;
I went to meet them at the road-side, bowing to them as they came.
But the moving horsemen did not hear that I spoke the Han tongue;
Their Captain took me for a Tartar born and had me bound in
    chains.
They are sending me away to the south-east, to a low and swampy
    land
Provided with hardly any kit and no protective drugs.
Thinking of this my voice chokes and I ask of Heaven above,
Was I spared from death only to spend the rest of my years in
    sorrow?
My native village in Liang plain I shall not see again;
My wife and children in the Tartars' land I have fruitlessly deserted.
When I fell among Tartars and was taken prisoner, I pined for the
    land of Han;
Now that I am back in the land of Han, they have turned me into a
    Tartar.

[1] In Kansu.
[2] A.D. 766-780.
[3] The Gobi Desert.
[4] The grave of Chao-chün, a Chinese girl who in 33 B.C. was 'bestowed upon the Khan of the Hsiung-nu as a mark of Imperial regard' (Giles). Hers was the only grave in this desolate district on which grass would grow.
[5] i.e. Chinese.

Had I but known what my fate would be, I would not have started
       home!
For the two lands, so wide apart, are alike in the sorrow they bring.
       Tartar prisoners in chains!
Of all the sorrows of all the prisoners mine is the hardest to bear!
Never in the world has so great a wrong fallen to the lot of man—
A Han heart and a Han tongue set in the body of a Turk.'

THE OLD MAN WITH THE BROKEN ARM

(A Satire on Militarism)

(c. A.D. 809)

At Hsin-fêng an old man—four-score and eight;
The hair on his head and the hair of his eyebrows—white as the new
       snow.
Leaning on the shoulders of his great-grandchildren, he walks in
       front of the Inn;
With his left arm he leans on their shoulders; his right arm is broken.
I asked the old man how many years had passed since he broke his
       arm;
I also asked the cause of the injury, how and why it happened?
The old man said he was born and reared in the District of Hsin-
       fêng;
At the time of his birth—a wise reign; no wars or discords.
'Often I listened in the Pear-Tree Garden to the sound of flute and
       song;
Naught I knew of banner and lance; nothing of arrow or bow.
Then came the wars of T'ien-pao[1] and the great levy of men;
Of three men in each house—one man was taken.
And those to whom the lot fell, where were they taken to?
Five months' journey, a thousand miles—away to Yün-nan.
We heard it said that in Yün-nan there flows the Lu River;
As the flowers fall from the pepper-trees, poisonous vapours rise.
When the great army waded across, the water seethed like a
       cauldron;
When barely ten had entered the water, two or three were dead.
To the north of my village, to the south of my village the sound of
       weeping and wailing,

A.D. 742-755.

Children parting from fathers and mothers; husbands parting from
  wives.
Everyone says that in expeditions against the Man tribes
Of a million men who are sent out, not one returns.
            I, that am old, was then twenty-four;
My name and fore-name were written down in the rolls of the Board
  of War.
In the depth of the night not daring to let anyone know
I secretly took a huge stone and dashed it against my arm.
For drawing the bow and waving the banner now wholly unfit
I knew henceforward I should not be sent to fight in Yün-nan.
Bones broken and sinews wounded could not fail to hurt;
My plan was to be rejected and sent back to my home.
My arm—broken ever since; it was sixty years ago.
One limb, although destroyed—whole body safe!
But even now on winter nights when the wind and rain blow
From evening on till day's dawn I cannot sleep for pain.
            Not sleeping for pain
            Is a small thing to bear,
Compared with the joy of being alive when all the rest are dead.
For otherwise, years ago, at the ford of Lu River
My body would have died and my soul hovered by the bones that
  no one gathered.
A ghost, I'd have wandered in Yün-nan, always looking for home.
Over the graves of ten thousand soldiers, mournfully hovering.'
            So the old man spoke,
            And I bid you listen to his words.
            Have you not heard
That the Prime Minister of K'ai-yüan,[1] His Excellency Sung,[2]
Did not reward frontier exploits, lest a spirit of aggression should
  prevail?
            And have you not heard
That the Prime Minister of T'ien-Pao, Yang Kuo-chung,[3]
Desiring to win imperial favour, started a frontier war,
But long before he could win the war, people had lost their temper?
Ask the man with the broken arm in the village of Hsin-fêng.

[1] 713-742.
[2] Sung Ying; died 737.
[3] Cousin of the notorious mistress of Ming-huang, Yang Kuei-fei.

THE FIVE-STRING[1]

THE singers have hushed their notes of shrill song;
The red sleeves of the dancers are motionless.
Old Chao[2] hugs his five-stringed lute;
Then his fingers dart, as he holds it close to his breast.
The loud notes swell and scatter abroad;
'Sa, sa', like wind blowing the rain.
The soft notes dying almost to nothing;
'Ch'ieh, ch'ieh', like the voice of ghosts talking.
Now as glad as the magpie's lucky song;
Again bitter as the gibbon's ominous cry.
His ten fingers have no fixed note;
Up and down—*kung, chih*, and *yü*.[3]
And those who sit and listen to the tune he plays
Of soul and body lose the mastery.
And those who pass that way as he plays the tune
Suddenly stop and cannot raise their feet.

Alas, alas that the ears of common men
Should love the modern and not love the old.
Thus it is that the lute in the green window
Day by day is covered deeper with dust.

THE FLOWER MARKET

IN the Royal City spring is almost over;
Tinkle, tinkle—the coaches and horsemen pass.
We tell each other 'This is the peony season';
And follow with the crowd that goes to the Flower Market.
'Cheap and dear—no uniform price;
The cost of the plant depends on the number of blossoms.
The flaming reds, a hundred on one stalk;
The humble white with only five flowers.
Above is spread an awning to protect them;
Around is woven a wattle-fence to screen them.
If you sprinkle water and cover the roots with mud,
When they are transplanted, they will not lose their beauty.'

[1] A kind of guitar imported from Bukhara.
[2] Chao Pi, a famous player of this instrument.
[3] Tonic, dominant and sixth of the pentatonic scale.

Each household thoughtlessly follows the custom,
Man by man, no one realizing.
There happened to be an old farm labourer
    Who came by chance that way.
He bowed his head and sighed a deep sigh;
But this sigh nobody understood.
He was thinking, 'A cluster of deep-red flowers
Would pay the taxes of ten poor houses.'

AT THE END OF SPRING

To Yüan Chên[1]

(A.D. 810)

THE flower of the pear-tree gathers and turns to fruit;
The swallows' eggs have hatched into young birds.
When the Seasons' changes thus confront the mind
What comfort can the Doctrine of Tao give?
It will teach me to watch the days and months fly
Without grieving that Youth slips away;
If the Fleeting World is but a long dream,
It does not matter whether one is young or old.
But ever since the day that my friend left my side
And has lived an exile in the City of Chiang-ling,
There is one wish I cannot quite destroy:
That from time to time we may chance to meet again.

THE POEM ON THE WALL

(A.D. 810)

Yüan Chên wrote that on his way to exile he had discovered a
poem inscribed by Po Chü-i on the wall of the Lo-k'ou Inn.

MY clumsy poem on the inn-wall none cared to see;
With bird-droppings and moss's growth the letters were blotched
    away.
There came a guest with heart so full, that though a page to the
    Throne,
He did not grudge with his broidered coat to wipe off the dust, and
    read.

[1] Po Chü-i's great friend. See pages 140, 144, 171.

AN EARLY LEVÉE

Addressed to Ch'ên, the Hermit

At Ch'ang-an—a full foot of snow;
A levée at dawn—to bestow congratulations on the Emperor.
Just as I was nearing the Gate of the Silver Terrace,
After I had left the ward of Hsin-ch'ang
On the high causeway my horse's foot slipped;
In the middle of the journey my lantern suddenly went out.
Ten leagues riding, always facing to the North;
The cold wind almost blew off my ears.
I waited for the bell outside the Five Gates;
I waited for the summons within the Triple Hall.
My hair and beard were frozen and covered with icicles;
My coat and robe—chilly like water.
Suddenly I thought of Hsien-yu Valley
And secretly envied Ch'ên Chü-shih,
In warm bed-socks dozing beneath the rugs
And not getting up till the sun has mounted the sky.

THE LETTER

(A.D. 810)

Preface.—After I parted with Yüan Chên, I suddenly dreamt one night that I saw him. When I awoke, I found that a letter from him had just arrived and, enclosed in it, a poem on the *paulovnia* flower.

We talked together in the Yung-shou Temple;
We parted to the north of the Hsin-ch'ang ward.
Going home—I shed a few tears,
Grieving about things—not sorry for you.
Long, long the Lan-t'ien road;
You said yourself you would not be able to write.
Reckoning up your halts for eating and sleeping—
By this time you've crossed the Shang mountains.
Last night the clouds scattered away;
A thousand leagues, the same moonlight scene.
When dawn came, I dreamt I saw your face;
It must have been that you were thinking of me.
In my dream, I thought I held your hand
And asked you to tell me what your thoughts were.

123

And *you* said: 'I miss you bitterly,
But there's no one here to send to you with a letter.'
When I awoke, before I had time to speak,
A knocking on the door sounded 'Doong, doong!'
They came and told me a messenger from Shang-chou
Had brought a letter—a single scroll from you!
Up from my pillow I suddenly sprang out of bed,
And threw on my clothes, all topsy-turvy.
I undid the knot and saw the letter within;
A single sheet with thirteen lines of writing.
At the top it told the sorrows of an exile's heart;
At the bottom it described the pains of separation.
The sorrows and pains took up so much space
There was no room left to talk about the weather!
But you said that when you wrote
You were staying for the night to the east of Shang-chou;
Sitting alone, lighted by a solitary candle
Lodging in the mountain hostel of Yang-ch'êng.
Night was late when you finished writing,
The mountain moon was slanting towards the west.
What is it lies aslant across the moon?
A single tree of purple paulovnia flowers—
Paulovnia flowers just on the point of falling
Are a symbol to express 'thinking of an absent friend'.
Lovingly—you wrote on the back side,
To send in the letter, your 'Poem of the Paulovnia Flower'.
The Poem of the Paulovnia Flower has eight rhymes;
Yet these eight couples have cast a spell on my heart.
They have taken hold of this morning's thoughts
And carried them to yours, the night you wrote your letter.
The whole poem I read three times;
Each verse ten times I recite.
So precious to me are the fourscore words
That each letter changes into a bar of gold!

GOLDEN BELLS

WHEN I was almost forty
I had a daughter whose name was Golden Bells.
Now it is just a year since she was born;
She is learning to sit and cannot yet talk.

124

Ashamed—to find that I have not a sage's heart;
I cannot resist vulgar thoughts and feelings.
Henceforward I am tied to things outside myself;
My only reward—the pleasure I am getting now.
If I am spared the grief of her dying young,
Then I shall have the trouble of getting her married.
My plan for retiring and going back to the hills
Must now be postponed for fifteen years!

CHU CH'ÊN VILLAGE

(In north-west Kiangsu)
(A.D. 811)

IN Hsü-chou, in the District of Ku-fêng
There lies a village whose name is Chu-ch'ên—
A hundred miles away from the county town,
Amid fields of hemp and green of mulberry-trees.
Click, click, the sound of the spinning-wheel;
Donkeys and oxen pack the village streets.
The girls go drawing the water from the brook;
The men go gathering fire-wood on the hill.
So far from the town Government affairs are few;
So deep in the hills, men's way are simple.
Though they have wealth, they do not traffic with it;
Though they reach the age, they do not enter the Army.
Each family keeps to its village trade;
Grey-headed, they have never left the gates.
Alive, they are the people of Ch'ên Village;
Dead, they become the dust of Ch'ên Village.
Out in the fields old men and young
Gaze gladly, each in the other's face.
In the whole village there are only two clans;
Age after age Chus have married Ch'êns.
Near or distant, they live in one clan;
Young or old, they move as one flock.
On white wine and brown fowl they fare
At joyful meetings more than 'once a week'.
While they are alive, they have no distant partings;
For marriage takes them no further than the next village.
When they are dead—no distant burial;
Round the village graves lie thick.

They are not troubled either about life or death;
They have no anguish either of body or soul.
And so it happens that they live to a ripe age
And great-great-grandsons are often seen.

I was born in the Realms of Etiquette;
In early years, unprotected and poor.
In vain I learnt to distinguish between Evil and Good;
Bringing myself only labour and toil.
The age we live in honours the Doctrine of Names;[1]
Scholars prize marriages and rank.
With these fetters I gyved my own hands;
Truly I became a much-deceived man.
At ten years old I learnt to read books;
At fifteen, I knew how to write prose.
At twenty I was made a Bachelor of Arts;
At thirty I became a Censor at the Court.
Above, the duty I owe to Prince and parents;
Below, the ties that bind me to wife and child.
The support of my family, the service of my country—
For these tasks my nature is not apt.
I reckon the time that I first left my home;
From then till now—fifteen Springs!
My lonely boat has twice sailed to Ch'u;
Four times through Ch'in my lean horse has passed.
I have walked in the morning with hunger in my face;
I have lain at night with a soul that could not rest.
East and West I have wandered without pause,
Hither and thither like a cloud adrift in the sky.
In the civil-war my old home was destroyed;
Of my flesh and blood many are scattered and parted.
North of the River, yes, and South of the River—
In both lands are the friends of all my life;
Life-friends whom I never see at all—
Whose deaths I hear of only after the lapse of years.
Sad at morning, I lie on my bed till dusk;
Weeping at night, I sit and wait for dawn.
The fire of sorrow has burnt my heart's core;
The frost of trouble has seized my hair's roots.
In such anguish my whole life has passed;
Long I have envied the people of Ch'ên Village.

---

[1] Confucianism.

FISHING IN THE WEI RIVER

(A.D. 811)

IN waters still as a burnished mirror's face,
In the depths of Wei, carp and grayling swim.
Idly I come with my bamboo fishing-rod
And hang my hook by the banks of Wei stream.
A gentle wind blows on my fishing-gear
Softly shaking my ten feet of line.
Though my body sits waiting for fish to come,
My heart has wandered to the Land of Nothingness.[1]
Long ago a white-headed man[2]
Also fished at the same river's side;
A hooker of men, not a hooker of fish,
At seventy years, he caught Wên Wang.[2]
But *I*, when I come to cast my hook in the stream,
Have no thought either of fish or men.
Lacking the skill to capture either prey,
I can only bask in the autumn water's light.
When I tire of this, my fishing also stops;
I go to my home and drink my cup of wine.

LAZY MAN'S SONG

(A.D. 811)

I COULD have a job, but am too lazy to choose it;
I have got land, but am too lazy to farm it.
My house leaks; I am too lazy to mend it.
My clothes are torn; I am too lazy to darn them.
I have got wine, but I am too lazy to drink;
So it's just the same as if my cup were empty.
I have got a lute, but am too lazy to play;
So it's just the same as if it had no strings.
My family tells me there is no more steamed rice;
I want to cook, but am too lazy to grind.
My friends and relatives write me long letters;

[1] See *Chuang Tzŭ*, ch. 1 end.
[2] The Sage T'ai-kung sat till he was seventy, apparently fishing, but really waiting for a prince who would employ him. At last Wên Wang, king of Chou, happened to come that way and at once made him his counsellor.

I should like to read them, but they're such a bother to open.
I have always been told that Hsi Shu-yeh[1]
Passed his whole life in absolute idleness.
But he played his lute and sometimes worked at his forge;
So even *he* was not so lazy as I.

WINTER NIGHT

Written during his retirement in 812

My house is poor; those that I love have left me.
My body is sick; I cannot join the feast.
There is not a living soul before my eyes
As I lie alone locked in my cottage room.
My broken lamp burns with a feeble flame;
My tattered curtains are crooked and do not meet.
'Tsek, tsek' on the door-step and window-sill
Again I hear the new snow fall.
As I grow older, gradually I sleep less;
I wake at midnight and sit up straight in bed.
If I had not learned the 'art of sitting and forgetting',[2]
How could I bear this utter loneliness?
Stiff and stark my body cleaves to the earth;
Unimpeded my soul yields to Change.[3]
So has it been for four tedious years,
Through one thousand and three hundred nights!

THE CHRYSANTHEMUMS IN THE EASTERN GARDEN

(A.D. 812)

The days of my youth left me long ago;
And now in their turn dwindle my years of prime.

---

[1] Hsi K'ang, see above, p. 73.

[2] Yen Hui told Confucius that he had acquired the 'art of sitting and forgetting'. Asked what that meant, Yen Hui replied: 'I have learnt to discard my body and obliterate my intelligence; to abandon matter and be impervious to sense-perception. By this method I become one with the All-pervading.'—*Chuang Tzŭ*, chap. vi.

[3] 'Change' is the principle of endless mutation which governs the Universe.

With what thoughts of sadness and loneliness
I walk again in this cold, deserted place!
In the midst of the garden long I stand alone;
The sunshine, faint; the wind and dew chill.
The autumn lettuce is tangled and turned to seed;
The fair trees are blighted and withered away.
All that is left are a few chrysanthemum-flowers
That have newly opened beneath the wattled fence.
I had brought wine and meant to fill my cup,
When the sight of these made me stay my hand.
    I remember, when I was young,
How quickly my mood changed from sad to gay.
If I saw wine, no matter at what season,
Before I drank it, my heart was already glad.
    But now that age comes
A moment of joy is harder and harder to get.
And always I fear that when I am quite old
The strongest liquor will leave me comfortless.
Therefore I ask you, late chrysanthemum-flower,
At this sad season why do you bloom alone?
Though well I know that it was not for my sake,
Taught by you, for a while I will smooth my frown.

THE TEMPLE

AUTUMN: the ninth year of Yüan Ho;[1]
The eighth month, and the moon swelling her arc.
It was then I travelled to the Temple of Wu-chên,
A temple terraced on Wang Shun's Hill.
While still the mountain was many leagues away,
Of scurrying waters we heard the plash and fret.
From here the traveller, leaving carriage and horse,
Begins to wade through the shallows of the Blue Stream,
His hand pillared on a green holly-staff,
His feet treading the torrent's white stones.
A strange quiet stole on ears and eyes,
That knew no longer the blare of the human world.
From mountain-foot gazing at mountain-top,
Now we doubted if indeed it could be climbed;

[1] A.D. 814

Who had guessed that a path deep hidden there
Twisting and bending crept to the topmost brow?
Under the flagstaff we made our first halt;
Next we rested in the shadow of the Stone Shrine.[1]
The shrine-room was scarce a cubit long,
With doors and windows unshuttered and unbarred.
I peered down, but could not see the dead;
Stalactites hung like a woman's hair.
Waked from sleep, a pair of white bats
Fled from the coffin with a whirr of snowy wings.
I turned away, and saw the Temple gate—
Scarlet eaves flanked by steeps of green;
'Twas as though a hand had ripped the mountain-side
And filled the cleft with a temple's walls and towers.
Within the gate, no level ground;
Little ground, but much empty sky.
Cells and cloisters, terraces and spires
High and low, followed the jut of the hill.
On rocky plateaux with no earth to hold
Were trees and shrubs, gnarled and very lean.
Roots and stems stretched to grip the stone;
Humped and bent, they writhed like a coiling snake.
In broken ranks pine and cassia stood,
Through the four seasons forever shady-green.
On tender twigs and delicate branches breathing
A quiet music played like strings in the wind.
Never pierced by the light of sun or moon,
Green locked with green, shade clasping shade.
A hidden bird sometimes softly sings;
Like a cricket's chirp sounds its muffled song.

At the Strangers' Arbour a while we stayed our steps;
We sat down, but had no mind to rest.
In a little while we had opened the northern door.
Ten thousand leagues suddenly stretched at our feet!
Brushing the eaves, shredded rainbows swept;
Circling the beams, clouds spun and whirled.
Through red sunlight white rain fell;
Azure and storm swam in a blended stream.
In a wild green clustered grasses and trees,
The eye's orbit swallowed the plain of Ch'in.

[1] Where the mummified bodies of priests were kept, in miniature temples.

Wei River was too small to see;
The Mounds of Han,[1] littler than a clenched fist.
I looked back; a line of red fence.
Broken and twisting, marked the way we had trod.
Far below, toiling one by one
Later climbers straggled on the face of the hill.

Straight before me were many Treasure Towers,
Whose wind-bells at the four corners sang.
At door and window, cornice and architrave
A thick cluster of gold and green-jade.
Some say that here the Buddha Kāśyapa[2]
Long ago quitted Life and Death.
Still they keep his iron begging-bowl,
With the furrow of his fingers chiselled deep at the base.
To the east there opens the jade Image Hall,
Where white Buddhas sit like serried trees.
We shook from our garments the journey's grime and dust,
And bowing worshipped those faces of frozen snow
Whose white cassocks like folded hoar-frost hung,
Whose beaded crowns glittered like a shower of hail.
We looked closer; surely Spirits willed
This handicraft, never chisel carved!
Next we climbed to the Chamber of Kuan-yin;[3]
From afar we sniffed its odours of sandal-wood.
At the top of the steps each doffed his shoes;
With bated stride we crossed the Jasper Hall.
The Jewelled Mirror on six pillars propped,
The Four Seats cased in hammered gold
Through the black night glowed with beams of their own,
Nor had we need to light candle or lamp.
These many treasures in concert nodded and swayed—
Banners of coral, pendants of cornaline.
When the wind came jewels chimed and sang
Softly, softly like the music of Paradise.
White pearls like frozen dewdrops hanging;
Dark rubies spilt like clots of blood,

[1] The tombs of the Han Emperors.
[2] Lived about 600,000,000,000 years ago and achieved Buddhahood at the age of 20,000.
[3] One of the self-denying Bodhisattvas who abstain from entering Buddhahood in order better to assist erring humanity. In Sanskrit, Avalokiteśvara.

Spangled and sown on the Buddha's twisted hair,
Together fashioned his Sevenfold Jewel-crown.
In twin vases of pallid tourmaline
(Their colour colder than the waters of an autumn stream)
The calcined relics of Buddha's Body rest—
Rounded pebbles, smooth as the Specular Stone.
A jade flute, by angels long ago
Borne as a gift to the Garden of Jetavan![1]
It blows a music sweet as the crane's song
That Spirits of Heaven earthward well might draw.

It was at autumn's height,
The fifteenth day and the moon's orbit full.
Wide I flung the three eastern gates;
A golden spectra walked at the chapel-door!
And now with moonbeams jewel-beams strove,
In freshness and beauty darting a crystal light
That cooled the spirit and limbs of all it touched,
Nor night-long needed they to rest.
At dawn I sought the road to the Southern Tope,
Where wild bamboos nodded in clustered grace.
In the lonely forest no one crossed my path;
Beside me faltered a cold butterfly.
Mountain fruits whose names I did not know
With their prodigal bushes hedged the pathway in;
The hungry here copious food had found;
Idly I plucked, to test sour and sweet.

South of the road, the Spirit of the Blue Dell,[2]
With his green umbrella and white paper pence!
When the year is closing, the people are ordered to grow,
As herbs of offering, marsil and motherwort;
So sacred the place, that never yet was stained
Its pure earth with sacrificial blood.

In a high cairn four or five rocks
Dangerously heaped, deep-scarred and heeling—
With what purpose did he that made the World
Pile them here at the eastern corner of the cliff!
Their slippery flank no foot has marked,

[1] Near Benares; here Buddha preached most of his Sūtras and the first
monastery was founded.
[2] A native, non-Buddhist deity.

132

But mosses stipple like a flowered writing-scroll.
I came to the cairn, I climbed it right to the top;
Beneath my feet a measureless chasm dropped.
My eyes were dizzy, hand and knee quaked—
I did not dare bend my head and look.
A boisterous wind rose from under the rocks,
Seized me with it and tore the ground from my feet.
My shirt and robe fanned like mighty wings,
And wide-spreading bore me like a bird to the sky.
High about me, triangular and sharp,
Like a cluster of sword-points many summits rose.
The white mist that struck them in its airy course
They tore asunder, and carved a patch of blue.

And now the sun was sinking in the north-west;
His evening beams from a crimson globe he shed,
Till far beyond the great fields of green
His sulphurous disk suddenly down he drove.

And now the moon was rising in the south-east;
In waves of coolness the night air flowed.
From the grey bottom of the hundred-fathom pool
Shines out the image of the moon's golden disk!
Blue as its name, the Lan River flows
Singing and plashing forever day and night.
I gazed down; like a green finger-ring
In winding circuits it follows the curves of the hill,
Sometimes spreading to a wide, lazy stream,
Sometimes striding to a foamy cataract.
Out from the deepest and clearest pool of all,
In a strange froth the Dragon's-spittle[1] flows.

I bent down; a dangerous ladder of stones
Paved beneath me a sheer and dizzy path.
I gripped the ivy, I walked on fallen trees,
Tracking the monkeys who came to drink at the stream.
Like a whirl of snowflakes the startled herons rose,
In damask dances the red sturgeon leapt.
For a while I rested, then plunging in the cool stream,
From my weary body I washed the stains away.
Deep or shallow, all was crystal clear;

[1] Ambergris.

133

I watched through the water my own thighs and feet.
Content I gazed at the stream's clear bed;
Wondered, but knew not, whence its waters flowed.

The eastern bank with rare stones is rife;
In serried courses the azure malachite,
That outward turns a smooth, glossy face;
In its deep core secret diamonds[1] lie.
Pien of Ch'u[2] died long ago,
And rare gems are often cast aside.
Sometimes a radiance leaks from the hill by night
To link its beams with the brightness of moon and stars.

At the central dome, where the hills highest rise,
The sky is pillared on a column of green jade;
Where even the spotty lizard cannot climb
Can I, a man, foothold hope to find?
In the top is hollowed the White-lotus lake;
With purple cusps the clear waves are crowned.
The name I heard, but the place I could not reach;
Beyond the region of mortal things it lies.

And standing here, a flat rock I saw,
Cubit-square, like a great paving-stone,
Midway up fastened in the cliff-wall;
And down below it, a thousand-foot drop.
Here they say that a Master in ancient days
Sat till he conquered the concepts of Life and Death.
The place is called the Settled Heart Stone;
By aged men the tale is still told.

I turned back to the Shrine of Fairies' Tryst;
Thick creepers covered its old walls.
Here it was that a mortal[3] long ago
On new-grown wings flew to the dark sky;
Westward a garden of agaric and rue
Faces the terrace where his magic herbs were dried.

[1] The stone mentioned (*yü-fan*), though praised by Confucius and used
in the ceremonies of his native state, cannot be identified. Its name evokes
vague ideas of rarity and beauty.
[2] Suffered mutilation because he had offered to his prince a gem which
experts rejected. Afterwards it turned out to be genuine.
[3] The wizard Wang Shun after whom the hill is named?

And sometimes still on clear moonlit nights
In the sky is heard a yellow-crane's voice.

I turned and sought the Painted Dragon Hall,
Where the bearded figures of two ancient men
By the Holy Lectern at sermon-time are seen
In gleeful worship to nod their hoary heads;
Who, going home to their cave beneath the river,
Of weather-dragons the writhing shapes assume
When rain is coming they puff a white smoke
In front of the steps, from a round hole in the stone.

Once a priest[1] who copied the Holy Books
(Of purpose dauntless and body undefiled)
Loved yonder pigeons, that far beyond the clouds
Fly in flocks beating a thousand wings.
They came and dropped him water in his writing-bowl;
Then sipped afresh in the river under the rocks.
Each day thrice they went and came,
Nor ever once missed their wonted time.
When the Book was finished they sent for a holy priest,
A disciple of his, named Yang-nan.
He sang the hymns of the Lotus Blossom Book,[2]
Again and again, a thousand, a million times.
His body perished, but his mouth still spoke,
The tongue resembling a red lotus-flower.
Today this relic is no longer shown;
But they still treasure the pyx in which it lies.

On a plastered wall are frescoes from the hand of Wu,[3]
Whose pencil-colours never-fading glow.
On a white screen is writing by the master Ch'u,[4]
    The tones subtle as the day it first dried.

Magical prospects, monuments divine—
Now all were visited.
Here we had tarried five nights and days;
Yet homeward now with loitering footsteps trod.
I, that a man of the wild hills was born,

---

[1] Fa-ch'êng, A.D. 563-640.
[2] The verses of the Saddharmapundarīka Sūtra, *Sacred Books of the East*, vol. 21.   [3] The great eighth-century painter, Wu Tao-tzŭ.
[4] The calligrapher, Ch'u Sui-liang, A.D. 596-658.

Floundering fell into the web of the World's net.
Caught in its trammels, they forced me to study books;
Twitched and tore me down the path of public life.
Soon I rose to be Bachelor of Arts;
In the Record Office, in the Censorate I sat.
My simple bluntness did not suit the times;
A profitless servant, I drew the royal pay.
The sense of this made me always ashamed,
And every pleasure a deep brooding dimmed.
To little purpose I sapped my heart's strength,
Till seeming age shrank my youthful frame.
From the very hour I doffed belt and cap
I marked how with them sorrow slank away.
But now that I wander in the freedom of streams and hills
My heart to its folly comfortably yields.
Like a wild deer that has torn the hunter's net
I range abroad by no halters barred.
Like a captive fish loosed into the Great Sea
To my marble basin I shall not ever return.
My body girt in the hermit's single dress,
My hands holding the Book of Chuang Chou,[1]
On these hills at last I am come to dwell,
Loosed forever from the shackles of a trim world.
I have lived in labour forty years and more;
If Life's remnant vacantly I spend,
Seventy being our span, then thirty years
Of idleness are still left to live.

ILLNESS AND IDLENESS

(A.D. 812)

ILLNESS and idleness give me much leisure.
What do I do with my leisure, when it comes?
I cannot bring myself to discard inkstone and brush;
Now and then I make a new poem.
When the poem is made, it is slight and flavourless,
A thing of derision to almost every one.
Superior people will be pained at the flatness of the metre;
Common people will hate the plainness of the words.

[1] See above, pp. 59, 127, 128.

I sing it to myself, then stop and think about it . . .

.   .   .   .

The Prefects of Soochow and P'êng-tsē[1]
Would perhaps have praised it, but they died long ago.
                    Who else would care to hear it?
No one to-day except Yüan Chên,
And *he* is banished to the City of Chiang-ling,
For three years a Clerk of Public Works.
Parted from me by three thousand leagues,
He will never know even that the poem was made.

POEMS IN DEPRESSION, AT WEI VILLAGE

(A.D. 812)

I

I HUG my pillow and do not speak a word;
In my empty room no sound stirs.
Who knows that, all day a-bed,
I am not ill and am not even asleep?

II

TURNED to jade are the boy's rosy cheeks;
To his sick temples the frost of winter clings. . . .
Do not wonder that my body sinks to decay;
Though my limbs are old, my heart is older yet.

ILLNESS

SAD, sad—lean with long illness;
Monotonous, monotonous—days and nights pass.
The summer trees have clad themselves in shade;
The autumn 'lan' already houses the dew.
The eggs that lay in the nest when I took to bed
Have changed into little birds and flown away.
The worm that then lay hidden in its hole

[1] Wei Ying-wu, eighth century A.D., and T'ao Ch'ien, A.D., 365-427.

137

Has hatched into a cricket sitting on the tree.
The Four Seasons go on for ever and ever;
In all Nature nothing stops to rest
Even for a moment. Only the sick man's heart
Deep down still aches as of old!

HERMIT AND POLITICIAN

'I WAS going to the City to sell the herbs I had plucked;
On the way I rested by some trees at the Blue Gate.
Along the road there came a horseman riding,
Whose face was pale with a strange look of dread.
Friends and relations, waiting to say good-bye,
Pressed at his side, but he did not dare to pause.
I, in wonder, asked the people about me
Who he was and what had happened to him.
They told me this was a Privy Councillor
Whose grave duties were like the pivot of State.
His food allowance was ten thousand cash;
Three times a day the Emperor came to his house.
Yesterday his counsel was sought by the Throne;
Today he is banished to the country of Yai-chou.[1]
So always, the Counsellors of Kings;
Favour and ruin changed between dawn and dusk!'

Green, green—the grass of the Eastern Suburb;
And amid the grass, a road that leads to the hills.
Resting in peace among the white clouds,
Can the hermit doubt that he chose the better part?

REJOICING AT THE ARRIVAL OF
CH'ÊN HSIUNG

(A.D. 814)

WHEN the yellow bird's note was almost stopped,
And half formed the green plum's fruit—
Sitting and grieving that spring things were over,
I rose and entered the Eastern Garden's gate.

[1] In the south of the island of Hainan, off Kwangtung.

138

I carried my cup and was dully drinking alone;
Suddenly I heard a knocking sound at the door.
Dwelling secluded, I was glad that someone had come;
How much the more, when I saw it was Ch'ên Hsiung!
At ease and leisure—all day we talked;
Crowding and jostling—the feelings of many years.
How great a thing is a single cup of wine!
For it makes us tell the story of our whole lives.

REMEMBERING GOLDEN BELLS

RUINED and ill—a man of two score;
Pretty and guileless—a girl of three.
Not a boy—but still better than nothing:
To soothe one's feeling—from time to time a kiss!
There came a day—they suddenly took her from me;
Her soul's shadow wandered I know not where.
And when I remember how just at the time she died
She lisped strange sounds, beginning to learn to talk,
Then I know that the ties of flesh and blood
Only bind us to a load of grief and sorrow.
At last, by thinking of the time before she was born,
By thought and reason I drove the pain away.
Since my heart forgot her, many days have passed
And three times winter has changed to spring.
This morning, for a little, the old grief came back,
Because, in the road, I met her foster-nurse.

KEPT WAITING IN THE BOAT AT CHIU-K'OU TEN DAYS BY AN ADVERSE WIND

(A.D. 815)

WHITE billows and huge waves block the river crossing;
Wherever I go, danger and difficulty; whatever I do, failure.
Just as in my worldly career I wander and lose the road,
So when I come to the river crossing, I am stopped by con-
    trary winds.

139

Of fishes and prawns sodden in the rain the smell fills my
    nostrils;
With the stings of insects that come with the fog my whole
    body is sore.
I am growing old, time flies, and my short span runs out,
While I sit in a boat at Chiu-k'ou,[1] wasting ten days!

ON BOARD SHIP:
READING YÜAN CHÊN'S POEMS

I TAKE your poems in my hand and read them beside the candle;
The poems are finished, the candle is low, dawn not yet come.
My eyes smart; I put out the lamp and go on sitting in the dark,
Listening to waves that, driven by the wind, strike the prow of the
    ship.

STARTING EARLY FROM THE
CH'U-CH'ÊNG INN

(A.D. 815)

WASHED by the rain, dust and grime are laid;
Skirting the river, the road's course is flat.
The moon has risen on the last remnants of night;
The travellers' speed profits by the early cold.
In the great silence I whisper a faint song;
In the black darkness are bred sombre thoughts.
On the lotus-bank hovers a dewy breeze;
Through the rice furrows trickles a singing stream.
At the noise of our bells a sleeping dog stirs;
At the sight of our torches a roosting bird wakes.
Dawn glimmers through the shapes of misty trees . . .
For ten miles, till day at last breaks.

[1] In central Hupeh, on the Han River.

ARRIVING AT HSÜN-YANG

(Two Poems)

I

A BEND of the river brings into view two triumphal arches;
That is the gate in the western wall of the suburbs of Hsün-yang.
I have still to travel in my solitary boat three or four leagues—
By misty waters and rainy sands, while the yellow dusk thickens.

II

We are almost come to Hsün-yang; how my thoughts are stirred
As we pass to the south of Yü Liang's tower and the east of P'ên Port.
The forest trees are leafless and withered—after the mountain rain;
The roofs of the houses are hidden low among the river mists.
The horses, fed on water grass, are too weak to carry their load;
The cottage walls of wattle and thatch let the wind blow on one's
    bed.
In the distance I see red-wheeled coaches driving from the town-
    gate;
They have taken the trouble, these civil people, to meet their new
    Prefect!

TO HIS BROTHER HSING-CHIEN, WHO WAS SERVING IN TUNG-CH'UAN

(Eastern Ssechuan)

(A.D. 815)

SULLEN, sullen, my brows are ever knit;
Silent, silent, my lips will not move.
It is not indeed that I choose to sorrow thus;
If I lift my eyes, who would share my joy?
Last Spring *you* were called to the West
To carry arms in the lands of Pa and Shu;
And this Spring *I* was banished to the South
To nurse my sickness on the River's oozy banks.
You are parted from me by six thousand leagues;
In another world, under another sky.
Of ten letters, nine do not reach;
What can I do to open my sad face?
Thirsty men often dream of drink;

Hungry men often dream of food.
Since Spring came where do my dreams lodge?
Ere my eyes are closed, I have travelled to Tung-ch'uan.

RAIN

(A.D. 815)

SINCE I lived a stranger in the City of Hsün-yang
Hour by hour bitter rain has poured.
On few days has the dark sky cleared;
In listless sleep I have spent much time.
The lake has widened till it almost joins the sky;
The clouds sink till they touch the water's face.
Beyond my hedge I hear the boatman's talk;
At the street-end I hear the fisher's song.
Misty birds are lost in yellow air;
Windy sails kick the white waves.
In front of my gate the horse and carriage-way
In a single night has turned into a river-bed.

RELEASING A MIGRANT 'YEN'
(WILD GOOSE)

AT Nine Rivers,[1] in the tenth year,[2] in winter—heavy snow;
The river-water covered with ice and the forests broken with their
    load.[3]
The birds of the air, hungry and cold, went flying east and west;
And with them flew a migrant 'yen', loudly clamouring for food.
Among the snow it pecked for grass, and rested on the surface of the
    ice;
It tried with its wings to scale the sky, but its tired flight was slow.
The boys of the river spread a net and caught the bird as it flew;
They took it in their hands to the city-market and sold it there alive.
I that was once a man of the North am now an exile here;
Bird and man, in their different kind, are each strangers in the south.
And because the sight of an exiled bird wounded an exile's heart,

[1] Kiukiang, the poet's place of exile.
[2] A.D. 815. His first winter at Kiukiang.
[3] By the weight of snow.

142

I paid your ransom and set you free, and you flew away to the clouds.

Yen, Yen, flying to the clouds, tell me, whither shall you go?
Of all things I bid you, do not fly to the land of the north-west.
In Huai-hsi there are rebel bands[1] that have not been subdued;
And a thousand thousand armoured men have long been camped in war.
The official army and the rebel army have grown old in their opposite trenches;
The soldier's rations have grown so small, they'll be glad of even you.
The brave boys, in their hungry plight, will shoot you and eat your flesh;
They will pluck from your body those long feathers and make them into arrow-wings!

THE BEGINNING OF SUMMER

(A.D. 815)

At the rise of summer a hundred beasts and trees
Join in gladness that the Season bids them thrive.
Stags and does frolic in the deep woods;
Snakes and insects are pleased by the rank grass.
Winged birds love the thick leaves;
Scaly fish enjoy the fresh weeds.
But to one place Summer forgot to come;
I alone am left like a withered straw . . .
In solitude, banished to the world's end;
Flesh and bone all in distant ways.
From my native place no tidings come;
Rebel troops flood the land with war.
Sullen grief, in the end, what will it bring?
I am only wearing my own heart away.
Better far to let both body and mind
Blindly yield to the fate that Heaven made.
Hsün-yang abounds in good wine;
I will fill my cup and never let it be dry.
On P'ên River fish are cheap as mud;
Early and late I will eat them, boiled and fried.

[1] The revolt of Wu Yüan-chi, put down in A.D. 817

143

With morning rice at the temple under the hill,
And evening wine at the island in the lake . . .
Why should my thoughts turn to my native land?
For in this place one could well end one's age.

HEARING THE EARLY ORIOLE

(c. A.D. 816)

WHEN the sun rose I was still lying in bed;
An early oriole sang on the roof of my house.
For a moment I thought of the Royal Park at dawn
When the birds of Spring greeted their Lord from his trees.
I remembered the days when I served before the Throne
Pencil in hand, on duty at the Ch'êng-ming;
At the height of spring, when I paused from drafting papers,
Morning and evening, was *this* the voice I heard?
Now in my exile the oriole sings again
In the dreary stillness of Hsün-yang town . . .
The bird's note cannot really have changed;
All the difference lies in the listener's heart.
If he could but forget that he lives at the world's end,
The bird would sing as it sang in the Palace of old.

DREAMING THAT I WENT WITH LI AND YÜ TO VISIT YÜAN CHÊN

(Written in exile)

AT night I dreamt I was back in Ch'ang-an;
I saw again the faces of old friends.
And in my dreams, under an April sky,
They led me by the hand to wander in the spring winds.
Together we came to the ward of Peace and Quiet;
We stopped our horses at the gate of Yüan Chên.
Yüan Chên was sitting all alone;
When he saw me coming, a smile came to his face.
He pointed back at the flowers in the western court;
Then opened wine in the northern summer-house.
He seemed to be saying that neither of us had changed;
He seemed to be regretting that joy will not stay;

That our souls had met only for a little while,
To part again with hardly time for greeting.
I woke up and thought him still at my side;
I put out my hand; there was nothing there at all.

MADLY SINGING IN THE MOUNTAINS

THERE is no one among men that has not a special failing;
And my failing consists in writing verses.
I have broken away from the thousand ties of life;
But this infirmity still remains behind.
Each time that I look at a fine landscape,
Each time that I meet a loved friend,
I raise my voice and recite a stanza of poetry
And marvel as though a God had crossed my path.
Ever since the day I was banished to Hsün-yang
Half my time I have lived among the hills.
And often, when I have finished a new poem,
Alone I climb the road to the Eastern Rock.
I lean my body on the banks of white Stone;
I pull down with my hands a green cassia branch.
My mad singing startles the valleys and hills;
The apes and birds all come to peep.
Fearing to become a laughing-stock to the world,
I choose a place that is unfrequented by men.

AFTER LUNCH

AFTER lunch—one short nap;
On waking up—two cups of tea.
Raising my head, I see the sun's light
Once again slanting to the south-west.
Those who are happy regret the shortness of the day;
Those who are sad tire of the year's sloth.
But those whose hearts are devoid of joy or sadness
Just go on living, regardless of 'short' or 'long'.

VISITING THE HSI-LIN TEMPLE

(A.D. 817)

I DISMOUNT from my horse at the Hsi-lin Temple;
I hurry forward, speeding with light cane.
In the morning I work at a Government office-desk;
In the evening I become a dweller in the Sacred Hills.
In the second month to the north of K'uang-lu
The ice breaks and the snow begins to melt.
On the southern plantation the tea-plant thrusts its sprouts;
Through the northern crevice the veins of the spring ooze.

.   .   .   .

This year there is war in An-hui,
In every place soldiers are rushing to arms.
Men of learning have been summoned to the Council Board;
Men of action are marching to the battle-line.
Only I, who have no talents at all,
Am left in the mountains to play with the pebbles of the stream.

EATING BAMBOO-SHOOTS

MY new Province is a land of bamboo-groves:
Their shoots in spring fill the valleys and hills.
The mountain woodman cuts an armful of them
And brings them down to sell at the early market.
Things are cheap in proportion as they are common;
For two farthings I buy a whole bundle.
I put the shoots in a great earthen pot
And heat them up along with boiling rice.
The purple skins broken—like an old brocade;
The white skin opened—like new pearls.
Now every day I eat them recklessly;
For a long time I have not touched meat.
All the time I was living at Lo-yang
They could not give me enough to suit my taste.
Now I can have as many shoots as I please;
For each breath of the south-wind makes a new bamboo!

TO A PORTRAIT PAINTER WHO
DESIRED HIM TO SIT

YOU, so bravely plying reds and blues
Just when I am getting wrinkled and old!
Why should you waste the moments of inspiration
Tracing the withered limbs of a sick man?
Tall, tall is the Palace of the Unicorn;[1]
But my deeds have not been frescoed on its walls.
Minutely limned on a foot of painting silk—
What can I do with a portrait such as that?

SEPARATION

YESTERDAY I heard that such-a-one was gone;
This morning they tell me that so-and-so is dead.
Of friends and acquaintances more than two-thirds
Have suffered change and passed to the Land of Ghosts.
Those that are gone I shall not see again;
They, alas, are for ever finished and done.
Those that are left—where are they now?
They are all scattered—a thousand miles away.
Those I have known and loved through all my life,
On the fingers of my hand—how many do I count?
Only the prefects of T'ung, Kuo and Li
And Fêng Province—just those four.[2]
Longing for each other we are all grown grey;
Through the Fleeting World rolled like a wave in the
        stream.
Alas that the feasts and frolics of old days
Have withered and vanished, bringing us to this!
When shall we meet and drink a cup of wine
And laughing gaze into each other's eyes?

[1] A sort of National Portrait Gallery.
[2] The Prefect of T'ung was Yüan Chên; the Prefect of Li was Li Chien
(died A.D. 821).

HAVING CLIMBED TO THE TOPMOST PEAK OF THE INCENSE-BURNER MOUNTAIN

UP and up, the Incense-burner Peak!
In my heart is stored what my eyes and ears perceived.
All the year—detained by official business;
Today at last I got a chance to go.
Grasping the creepers, I clung to dangerous rocks;
My hands and feet—weary with groping for hold.
There came with me three or four friends,
But two friends dared not go further.
At last we reached the topmost crest of the Peak;
My eyes were blinded, my soul rocked and reeled.
The chasm beneath me—ten thousand feet;
The ground I stood on, only a foot wide.
If you have not exhausted the scope of seeing and hearing,
How can you realize the wideness of the world?
The waters of the River looked narrow as a ribbon,
P'ên Castle smaller than a man's fist.
How it clings, the dust of the world's halter!
It chokes my limbs; I cannot shake it away.
Coming home I thought this over and sighed;
Then, with lowered head, came back to the Ants' Nest.

THE FIFTEENTH VOLUME

(Having completed the fifteenth volume of his works, the poet sends it to his friends, Yüan Chên and Li Shên, with a jesting poem.)

(Written in 818)

MY long poem, the 'Eternal Grief',[1] is a beautiful and moving work;
My ten 'Songs of Shensi' are models of tunefulness.
I cannot prevent Old Yüan from stealing my best rhymes;
But Little Li by a bitter lesson has learnt respect for my songs.
While I am alive, riches and honour will never fall to my lot;
But well I know that after I am dead the fame of my books will live.
This random talk and foolish boasting forgive me, for today
I have added Volume Fifteen to the row that stands to my name.

[1] See Giles, *Chinese Literature*, p. 169.

ALARM AT FIRST ENTERING THE YANG-TZE GORGES

(Written in A.D. 819, when he was being towed up the rapids
to Chung-chou, in Ssechwan)

ABOVE, a mountain ten thousand feet high;
Below, a river a thousand fathoms deep.
A strip of sky, walled by cliffs of stone;
Wide enough for the passage of a single reed.[1]
At Chü-t'ang a straight cleft yawns;
At Yen-yü islands block the stream.
Long before night the walls are black with dusk;
Without wind white waves rise.
The big rocks are like a flat sword;
The little rocks resemble ivory tusks.

———

We are stuck fast and cannot move a step.
How much the less, three hundred miles?[2]
Frail and slender, the twisted-bamboo rope;
Weak, the treacherous hold of the punters' feet.
A single slip—the whole convoy lost;
And *my* life hangs on *this* thread!
I have heard a saying 'He that has an upright heart
Shall walk scatheless through the lands of Man and Mo.'[3]
How can I believe that since the world began
In every shipwreck none have drowned but rogues?
And how can I, born in evil days
And fresh from failure, ask a kindness of Fate?
Often I fear that these un-talented limbs
Will be laid at last in an un-named grave!

[1] See *The Book of Songs*, p. 48.
[2] The distance to Chung-chou.
[3] Dangerous savages.

ON BEING REMOVED FROM
HSÜN-YANG AND SENT
TO CHUNG-CHOU

BEFORE this, when I was stationed at Hsün-yang,
Already I regretted the fewness of friends and guests.
Suddenly, suddenly—bearing a stricken heart
I left the gates, with nothing to comfort me.
Henceforward—relegated to deep seclusion
In a bottomless gorge, flanked by precipitous mountains.
Five months on end the passage of boats is stopped
By the piled billows that toss and leap like colts.
The inhabitants of Pa resemble wild apes;
Fierce and lusty, they fill the mountains and prairies.
Among such as these I cannot hope for friends
And am pleased with anyone who is even remotely human.

PLANTING FLOWERS ON THE
EASTERN EMBANKMENT

(Written when Governor of Chung-chou)

(A.D. 819)

I TOOK money and brought flowering trees
And planted them out on the bank to the east of the Keep.
I simply bought whatever had most blooms,
Not caring whether peach, apricot, or plum.
A hundred fruits, all mixed up together;
A thousand branches, flowering in due rotation.
Each has its season coming early or late;
But to all alike the fertile soil is kind.
The red flowers hang like a heavy mist;
The white flowers gleam like a fall of snow.
The wandering bees cannot bear to leave them;
The sweet birds also come there to roost.
In front there flows an ever-running stream;
Beneath there is built a little flat terrace.
Sometimes I sweep the flagstones of the terrace;
Sometimes, in the wind, I raise my cup and drink.
The flower-branches screen my head from the sun;
The flower-buds fall down into my lap.

Alone drinking, alone singing my songs
I do not notice that the moon is level with the steps.
The people of Pa do not care for flowers;
All the spring no one has come to look.
But their Governor General, alone with his cup of wine,
Sits till evening and will not move from the place!

INVITATION TO HSIAO CH'U-SHIH

(Written when Governor of Chung-chou)

WITHIN the Gorges there is no lack of men;
They are people one meets, not people one cares for.
At my front door guests also arrive;
They are people one sits with, not people one knows.
When I look up, there are only clouds and trees;
When I look down—only my wife and child.
I sleep, eat, get up or sit still;
Apart from that, nothing happens at all.
But beyond the city Hsiao the hermit dwells,
And with *him* at least I find myself at ease.
For *he* can drink a full flagon of wine
And is good at reciting long-line poems.
Some afternoon, when the clerks have gone home,
At a season when the path by the river bank is dry,
I beg you, take up your staff of bamboo-wood
And find your way to the parlour of Government House.

TO LI CHIEN

(A.D. 819)

THE province I govern is humble and remote;
Yet our festivals follow the Courtly Calendar.
At rise of day we sacrificed to the Wind God,
When darkly, darkly, dawn glimmered in the sky.
Officers followed, horsemen led the way;
They brought us out to the wastes beyond the town,
Where river mists fall heavier than rain,
And the fires on the hill leap higher than the stars

Suddenly I remembered the early levees at Court
When you and I galloped to the Purple Yard.
As we walked our horses up Dragon Tail Way
We turned and gazed at the green of the Southern Hills.
Since we parted, both of us have been growing old;
And our minds have been vexed by many anxious cares;
Yet even now I fancy my ears are full
Of the sound of jade tinkling on your bridle-straps.

THE RED COCKATOO

(A.D. 820)

SENT as a present from Annam—
A red cockatoo.
Coloured like the peach-tree blossom,
Speaking with the speech of men.
And they did to it what is always done
To the learned and eloquent.
They took a cage with stout bars
And shut it up inside.

THE SPRING RIVER

HEAT and cold, dusk and dawn have crowded one upon the other;
Suddenly I find it is two years since I came to Chung-chou.
Through my closed doors I hear nothing but the morning and
   evening drum;
From my upper windows all I see is the ships that come and go.
In vain the orioles tempt me with their song to stray beneath the
   flowering trees;
In vain the grasses lure me by their colour to sit beside the pond.
There is one thing and one alone I never tire of watching—
The spring river as it trickles over the stones and babbles past the
   rocks.

AFTER COLLECTING THE
AUTUMN TAXES

FROM these high walls I look at the town below
Where the natives of Pa cluster like a swarm of flies.
How can I govern these people and lead them aright?
I cannot even understand what they say.
But at least I am glad, now that the taxes are in,
To learn that in my province there is no discontent.
I fear its prosperity is not due to me
And was only caused by the year's abundant crops.
The papers I have to deal with are simple and few;
My arbour by the lake is leisurely and still.
In the autumn rain the berries fall from the eaves;
At the evening bell the birds return to the wood.
A broken sunlight quavers over the southern porch
Where I lie on my couch abandoned to idleness.

LODGING WITH THE OLD MAN OF
THE STREAM

(A.D. 820)

MEN'S hearts love gold and jade;
Men's mouths covet wine and flesh.
Not so the old man of the stream;
He drinks from his gourd and asks nothing more.
South of the stream he cuts firewood and grass;
North of the stream he has built wall and roof.
Yearly he sows a single acre of land;
In spring he drives two yellow calves.
In these things he finds great repose;
Beyond these he has no wish or care.
By chance I met him walking by the water-side;
He took me home and lodged me in his thatched hut.
When I parted from him, to seek market and Court,
This old man asked my rank and pay.
Doubting my tale, he laughed loud and long:
'Privy Counsellors do not sleep in barns.'

TO HIS BROTHER HSING-CHIEN

(A.D. 820)

       CAN the single cup of wine
We drank this morning have made my heart so glad?
This is a joy that comes only from within,
Which those who witness will never understand.
       I have but two brothers
And bitterly grieved that both were far away;
This spring, back through the Gorges of Pa,
I have come to them safely, ten thousand leagues.
       Two cousins I had
Who had put up their hair, but not twined the sash;[1]
Yesterday both were married and taken away
By good husbands in whom I may well trust.
I am freed at last from the thoughts that made me grieve,
As though a sword had cut a rope from my neck.
And limbs grow light when the heart sheds its care;
Suddenly I seem to be flying up to the sky!

     .   .   .   .   .

Hsing-chien, drink your cup of wine,
Then set it down and listen to what I say.
Do not sigh that your home is far away;
Do not mind if your salary is small.
Only pray that as long as life lasts
You and I may never be forced to part.

CHILDREN

(Written c. 820)

MY nephew, who is six years old, is called 'Tortoise';[2]
My daughter of three—little 'Summer Dress'.
One is beginning to learn to joke and talk;
The other can already recite poems and songs.
At morning they play clinging about my feet;
At night they sleep pillowed against my dress.

        [1] i.e. got married.
        [2] This is the 'Kuei' of p. 158.

Why, children, did you reach the world so late,
Coming to me just when my years are spent?
Young things draw our feelings to them;
Old people easily give their hearts.
The sweetest vintage at last turns sour;
The full moon in the end begins to wane.
And so with men the bonds of love and affection
Soon may change to a load of sorrow and care.
But all the world is bound by love's ties;
Why did I think that I alone should escape?

PRUNING TREES

TREES growing—right in front of my window;
The trees are high and the leaves grow thick.
Sad alas! the distant mountain view,
Obscured by this, dimly shows between.
One morning I took knife and axe;
With my own hand I lopped the branches off.
Ten thousand leaves fell about my head;
A thousand hills came before my eyes.
Suddenly, as when clouds or mists break
And straight through, the blue sky appears.
Again, like the face of a friend one has loved
Seen at last after an age of parting.
First there came a gentle wind blowing;
One by one the birds flew back to the tree.
To ease my mind I gazed to the South-East;
As my eyes wandered, my thoughts went far away.
Of men there is none that has not some preference;
Of things there is none but mixes good with ill.
It was not that I did not love the tender branches;
But better still—to see the green hills!

BEING VISITED BY A FRIEND
DURING ILLNESS

I HAVE been ill so long that I do not count the days;
At the southern window, evening—and again evening.

Sadly chirping in the grasses under my eaves
The winter sparrows morning and evening sing.
By an effort I rise and lean heavily on my bed;
Tottering I step towards the door of the courtyard.
By chance I meet a friend who is coming to see me;
Just as if I had gone specially to meet him.
They took my couch and placed it in the setting sun;
They spread my rug and I leaned on the balcony-pillar.
Tranquil talk was better than any medicine;
Gradually the feelings came back to my numbed heart.

THE PINE-TREES IN THE COURTYARD

(A.D. 821)

BELOW the Hall what meets my eyes?
Ten pine-trees growing near to the steps.
Irregularly scattered, not in ordered line;
In height also strangely unassorted.
The highest of them is thirty feet tall;
The lowest scarcely measures ten feet.
They have the air of things growing wild;
Who first planted them, no one now knows.
They touch the walls of my blue-tiled house;
Their roots are sunk in the terrace of white sand.
Morning and evening they are visited by the wind and moon;
Rain or fine—they are free from dust and mud.
In the gales of autumn they whisper a vague tune;
From the suns of summer they yield a cool shade.
At the height of spring the fine evening rain
Fills their leaves with a load of hanging pearls.
At the year's end the time of great snow
Stamps their branches with a fret of glittering jade.
At each season they have their varying mood;
Vying in this with any tree that grows.
Last year, when they heard I had bought this house,
Neighbours mocked and the World called me mad—
That a whole family of twice ten souls
Should move house for the sake of a few pines!
Now that I have come to them, what have they given me?

They have only loosened the shackles that bind my heart.
But even so, they are 'profitable friends',[1]
And fill my need of 'converse with wise men'.
Yet when I consider how, still a man of the world,
In belt and cap I scurry through dirt and dust,
From time to time my heart twinges with shame
That I am not fit to be master of my pines!

ON THE WAY TO HANGCHOW:
ANCHORED ON THE RIVER AT NIGHT

LITTLE sleeping and much grieving—the traveller
Rises at midnight and looks back towards home.
The sands are bright with moonlight that joins the shores;
The sail is white with dew that has covered the boat.
Nearing the sea, the river grows broader and broader
Approaching autumn—the nights longer and longer.
Thirty times we have slept amid mists and waves,
And still we have not reached Hangchow!

SLEEPING ON HORSEBACK

(A.D. 822)

WE had ridden long and were still far from the inn;
My eyes grew dim; for a moment I fell asleep.
Under my right arm the whip still dangled;
In my left hand the reins for an instant slackened.
Suddenly I woke and turned to question my groom.
'We have gone a hundred paces since you fell asleep.'
Body and spirit for a while had changed place;
Swift and slow had turned to their contraries.
For these few steps that my horse had carried me
Had taken in my dream countless aeons of time!
True indeed is that saying of Wise Men
'A hundred years are but a moment of sleep.'·

[1] See my *Analects of Confucius*, p. 205, where three kinds of 'profitable friends' and three kinds of 'profitable pleasures' are described; the third of the latter being 'plenty of intelligent companions'.

PARTING FROM THE WINTER STOVE

(A.D. 822)

On the fifth day after the rise of Spring,
Everywhere the season's gracious attitudes!
The white sun gradually lengthening its course,
The blue-grey clouds hanging as though they would fall;
The last icicle breaking into splinters of jade:
The new stems marshalling red sprouts.
The things I meet are all full of gladness;
It is not only *I* who love the Spring.
To welcome the flowers I stand in the back garden;
To enjoy the sunlight I sit under the front eaves.
Yet still in my heart there lingers one regret;
Soon I shall part with the flame of my red stove!

THE SILVER SPOON

(While on the road to his new province, Hangchow, in 822,
he sent a silver spoon to his nephew A-kuei, whom he had been
obliged to leave behind with his nurse, old Mrs Tsou.)

To distant service my heart is well accustomed;
When I left home, it wasn't that which was difficult
But because I had to leave Kuei at home—
For this it was that tears filled my eyes.
Little boys ought to be daintily fed:
Mrs Tsou, please see to this!
That's why I've packed and sent a silver spoon;
You will think of me and eat up your food nicely!

THE HAT GIVEN TO THE POET BY
LI CHIEN

(Died, A.D. 821)

Long ago to a white-haired gentleman
You made the present of a black gauze hat.
The gauze hat still sits on my head;
But you already are gone to the Nether Springs.

The thing is old, but still fit to wear;
The man is gone and will never be seen again.
Out on the hill the moon is shining tonight
And the trees on your tomb are swayed by the autumn
    wind.

GOOD-BYE TO THE PEOPLE
OF HANGCHOW

(A.D. 824)

ELDERS and officers line the returning road;
Flagons of wine load the parting table.
I have not ruled you with the wisdom of Shao Kung;[1]
What is the reason your tears should fall so fast?
My taxes were heavy, though many of the people were poor;
The farmers were hungry, for often their fields were dry.
All I did was to dam the water of the Lake[2]
And help a little in a year when things were bad.

AFTER GETTING DRUNK, BECOMING
SOBER IN THE NIGHT

OUR party scattered at yellow dusk and I came home to bed;
I woke at midnight and went for a walk, leaning heavily on a friend.
As I lay on my pillow my vinous complexion, soothed by sleep,
    grew sober:
In front of the tower the ocean moon, accompanying the tide, had
    risen.
The swallows, about to return to the beams, went back to roost
    again;
The candle at my window, just going out, suddenly revived its light.
All the time till dawn came, still my thoughts were muddled;
And in my ears something sounded like the music of flutes and
    strings.

[1] A legendary ruler who dispensed justice sitting under a wild pear-tree.
[2] Po Chü-i built the dam on the Western Lake which is still known as
'Po's dam'.

WRITTEN WHEN GOVERNOR
OF SOOCHOW

(A.D. 825)

A Government building, not my own home.
A Government garden, not my own trees.
But at Lo-yang I have a small house,
And on Wei River I have built a thatched hut.
I am free from the ties of marriage and giving in marriage;
If I choose to retire, I have somewhere to end my days.
And though I have lingered long beyond my time,
To retire now would be better than not at all!

GETTING UP EARLY ON A
SPRING MORNING

(Part of a poem written when Governor of Soochow in 825)

THE early light of the rising sun shines on the beams of my house;
The first banging of opened doors echoes like the roll of a drum.
The dog lies curled on the stone step, for the earth is wet with dew;
The birds come near to the window and chatter, telling that the day
     is fine.
With the lingering fumes of yesterday's wine my head is still
     heavy;
With new doffing of winter clothes my body has grown light.
I woke up with heart empty and mind utterly extinct;
Lately, for many nights on end, I have not dreamt of home.

STOPPING THE NIGHT AT
JUNG-YANG

I GREW up near the town of Jung-yang.[1]
I was still young when I left my village home.
On and on—forty years passed
Till again I stayed for the night at Jung-yang.
When I went away, I was only eleven or twelve;
This year I am turned fifty-six.

[1] In Honan, near K'ai-fêng.

Yet thinking back to the times of my childish games,
Whole and undimmed, still they rise before me.
The old houses have all disappeared;
Down in the village none of my people are left.
It is not only that streets and buildings have changed;
But steep is level and level changed to steep!
Alone unchanged, the waters of Chên and Wei
Passionless—flow in their old course.[1]

RESIGNATION

Part of a Poem

(A.D. 826)

KEEP off your thoughts from things that are past and done;
For thinking of the past wakes regret and pain.
Keep off your thoughts from thinking what will happen;
To think of the future fills one with dismay.
Better by day to sit like a sack in your chair;
Better by night to lie like a stone in your bed.
When food comes, then open your mouth;
When sleep comes, then close your eyes.

CLIMBING THE TERRACE OF KUAN-YIN AND LOOKING AT THE CITY OF CH'ANG-AN

(A.D. 827)

HUNDREDS of houses, thousands of houses—like a great chess-board.
The twelve streets like a huge field planted with rows of cabbage.
In the distance I see faint and small the torches of riders to Court,
Like a single row of stars lying to the west of the Five Gates.

[1] Ever since the far-off days of the *Book of Songs* (see my translation, p. 45).

CLIMBING THE LING-YING TERRACE
AND LOOKING NORTH

Mounting on high I begin to realize the smallness of Man's
    Domain;
Gazing into distance I begin to know the vanity of the Carnal
    World.
I turn my head and hurry home—back to the Court and Market,
A single grain of rice falling—into the Great Barn.

REALIZING THE FUTILITY OF LIFE

(Written on the wall of a priest's cell, *circa* 828)

Ever since the time when I was a lusty boy
Down till now when I am ill and old,
The things I have cared for have been different at different
    times,
But my being busy, *that* has never changed.
Then on the shore—building sand-pagodas.
Now, at Court, covered with tinkling jade.
This and that—equally childish games,
Things whose substance passes in a moment of time!
While the hands are busy, the heart cannot understand;
When there is no Attachment, Doctrine is sound.
Even should one zealously strive to learn the Way,
That very striving will make one's error more.

THE GRAND HOUSES AT LO-YANG

(*c.* A.D. 829)

By woods and water, whose houses are these
With high gates and wide-stretching lands?
From their blue gables gilded fishes hang;
By their red pillars carven coursers run.
Their spring arbours, warm with caged mist;
Their autumn yards with locked moonlight cold.
To the stem of the pine-tree amber beads cling;

The bamboo-branches ooze ruby-drops.
Of lake and terrace who may the masters be?
High officers, Councillors-of-State.
All their lives they have never come to see,
But know their houses only from the bailiff's map!

THE HALF-RECLUSE

(A.D. 829)

'THE great recluse lives in market and court;
The small recluse hides in thickets and hills.'
Thickets and hills are too lonely and cold;
Market and court are too unrestful and thronged.
Far better to be a half-recluse,
And hermitize in a liaison job.
It is like office, yet like being at large;
One is not busy, but also not bored.
It makes no demand either on hand or brain,
Yet still prevents one being hungry or cold.
All the year one has no official work,
Yet every month one draws rations and pay.
For one who likes to take a strenuous climb
To the South of the city there are pleasant autumn hills;
For one who loves to take an idle stroll
To the East of the city are orchards lovely in spring.
If once in a while you want to get drunk
You can always accept an invitation to dine.
In Lo-Yang there are many delightful people
Always ready for endless pleasant talk.
But if you would rather lie quietly at home
All you need do is to bar your outer door;
There is no fear that official coaches or chairs
Will press for admittance, crowding in front of your gate
It is well known that life being what it is
To have things both ways is always very hard.
The lot of the humble is embittered by hunger and cold;
The great are compassed by many worries and cares.
Only the half-hermit of whom I speak
Achieves a life that is fortunate and secure.

163

Failure, success, affluence and want—
At an equal distance from all these four.

(Written when he was Lo-yang *liaison* to the Crown Prince's
Social Secretary.)

THE CRANES

(A.D. 830)

THE western wind has blown but a few days;
Yet the first leaf already flies from the bough.
On the drying paths I walk in my thin shoes;
In the first cold I have donned my quilted coat.
Through shallow ditches the floods are clearing away;
Through sparse bamboos trickles a slanting light.
In the early dusk, down an alley of green moss,
The garden-boy is leading the cranes home.

RISING LATE, AND PLAYING WITH A-TS'UI, AGED TWO

(Written in 831)

ALL the morning I have lain snugly in bed;
Now at dusk I rise with many yawns.
My warm stove is quick to get ablaze;
At the cold mirror I am slow in doing my hair.
With melted snow I boil fragrant tea;
Seasoned with curds I cook a milk-pudding.
At my sloth and greed there is no one but me to laugh;
My cheerful vigour none but myself knows.
The taste of my wine is mild and works no poison;
The notes of my lute are soft and bring no sadness.
To the Three Joys in the book of Mencius[1]
I have added the fourth of playing with my baby-boy.

[1] *Mencius*, Bk. vii, pt. i, 20.

ON BEING SIXTY

BETWEEN thirty and forty one is distracted by the Five Lusts;
Between seventy and eighty one is prey to a hundred diseases.
But from fifty to sixty one is free from all ills;
Calm and still—the heart enjoys rest.
I have put behind me Love and Greed, I have done with Profit and
　　Fame;
I am still short of illness and decay, and far from decrepit age.
Strength of limb I still possess to seek the rivers and hills;
Still my heart has spirit enough to listen to flutes and strings.
At leisure I open new wine and taste several cups;
Drunken I recall old poems and chant a stray verse.
To Tun-shih and Mêng-tê[1] I offer this advice:
Do not complain of three-score, 'the time of obedient ears.'[2]

ON HIS BALDNESS

(A.D. 832)

AT dawn I sighed to see my hairs fall;
At dusk I sighed to see my hairs fall.
For I dreaded the time when the last lock should go . . .
They are all gone and I do not mind at all!
I have done with that cumbrous washing and getting dry;
My tiresome comb for ever is laid aside.
Best of all, when the weather is hot and wet,
To have no top-knot weighing down on one's head!
I put aside my messy cloth wrap;
I have got rid of my dusty tasselled fringe.
In a silver jar I have stored a cold stream,
On my bald pate I trickle a ladle full.
Like one baptized with the Water of Buddha's Law,
I sit and receive this cool, cleansing joy.
Now I know why the priest who seeks Repose
Frees his heart by first shaving his head.

---

[1] Ts' ui Ch'ün and Liu Yü-hsi, who were the same age as Po Chü-i.
[2] Confucius said that not till sixty did 'his ears obey him'.

LOSING A SLAVE-GIRL

(A.D. 832)

AROUND my courtyard the little wall is low;
At the street door her loss was posted late.
I am ashamed to think we were not always kind;
I regret your labours, that will never be repaid.
The caged bird owes no allegiance;
The wind-tossed flower does not cling to the tree.

     •   •   •   •

Where tonight she lies none can give us news;
Nor any knows, save the bright watching moon.

THINKING OF THE PAST

(A.D. 833)

IN an idle hour I thought of former days
And former friends seemed to be standing in the room.
And then I wondered 'Where are they now?'
Like fallen leaves they have tumbled to the Nether Springs.
Han Yü[1] swallowed his sulphur pills,
Yet a single illness carried him straight to the grave.
Yüan Chên smelted autumn stone,[2]
But before he was old, his strength crumbled away.
Master Tu possessed a cinnabar receipt;
All day long he fasted from strong meats.
The Lord Ts'ui, trusting in the power of drugs,
Through the whole winter wore his summer coat.
Yet some by illness and some by sudden death . . .
All vanished ere their middle years were passed.

Only I, who never dieted myself,
Have succeeded in living to a ripe old age.
                     I who in young days
Yielded lightly to every lust and greed;
Whose palate craved only for the richest meat
And knew nothing of mercury or lead.

[1] The famous poet, died A.D. 824.
[2] Carbamide crystals.

166

When hunger came, I gulped steaming food;
When thirst came, I drank from the frozen stream.
With verse I laboured the spirits of my Five Guts;[1]
With wine I deluged the three Vital Spots.
Yet day by day joining fissures and breaks
I have lived till now almost sound and whole.
There is no gap in my two rows of teeth;
Limbs and body still serve me well.
Already I have opened my seventh set of years;
Yet I eat my fill and sleep quietly.
I drink, while I may, the wine that lies in my cup,
And all else commit to Heaven's care.

ON A BOX CONTAINING HIS OWN WORKS

(A.D. 835)

I BREAK up cypress and make a book-box;
The box well-made—and the cypress-wood tough.
In it shall be kept what author's works?
The inscription says Po Lo-t'ien.
All my life has been spent in writing books,
From when I was young till now that I am old.
First and last—seventy whole volumes;
Big and little—three thousand themes.
Well I know in the end they'll be scattered and lost;
But I cannot bear to see them thrown away.
With my own hand I open and shut the locks,
And put it carefully in front of the book-curtain.
I am like Têng Pai-tao;[2]
But to-day there is not any Wang Ts'an.[3]
All I can do is to divide them among my daughters
To be left by them to give to my grandchildren.

[1] Heart, liver, stomach, lungs, and kidneys.
[2] Who died childless in A.D. 326.
[3] To whom Ts'ai Yung (died A.D. 192) bequeathed his writings.

A MAD POEM ADDRESSED TO MY NEPHEWS AND NIECES

(A.D. 835)

THE World cheats those who cannot read;
I, happily, have mastered script and pen.
The World cheats those who hold no office;
I am blessed with high official rank.
Often the old have much sickness and pain;
With me, luckily, there is not much wrong.
People when they are old are often burdened with ties;
But *I* have finished with marriage and giving in marriage.
No changes happen to jar the quiet of my mind;
No business comes to impair the vigour of my limbs.
Hence it is that now for ten years
Body and soul have rested in hermit peace.
And all the more, in the last lingering years
What I shall need are very few things.
A single rug to warm me through the winter;
One meal to last me the whole day.
It does not matter that my house is rather small;
One cannot sleep in more than one room!
It does not matter that I have not many horses;
One cannot ride on two horses at once!
As fortunate as me among the people of the world
Possibly one would find seven out of ten.
As contented as me among a hundred men
Look as you may, you will not find one.
In the affairs of others even fools are wise;
In their own business even sages err.
To no one else would I dare to speak my heart,
So my wild words are addressed to my nephews and
    nieces.

OLD AGE

(Addressed to Liu Yü-hsi, who was born in the same year)

(A.D. 835)

WE are growing old together, you and I;
Let us ask ourselves, what is age like?

168

The dull eye is closed ere night comes;
The idle head, still uncombed at noon.
Propped on a staff, sometimes a walk abroad;
Or all day sitting with closed doors.
One dares not look in the mirror's polished face;
One cannot read small-letter books.
Deeper and deeper, one's love of old friends;
Fewer and fewer, one's dealings with young men.
One thing only, the pleasure of idle talk,
Is great as ever, when you and I meet.

EASE

*(Congratulating himself on the comforts of his life during a
temporary retirement from office. A.D. 835)*

LINED coat, warm cap and easy felt slippers,
In the little tower, at the low window, sitting over the sunken
  brazier.
Body at rest, heart at peace; no need to rise early.
I wonder if the courtiers at the Western Capital know of these
  things, or not?

TO A TALKATIVE GUEST

(A.D. 836)

THE town visitor's easy talk flows in an endless stream;
The country host's quiet thoughts ramble timidly on.
'I beg you, Sir, do not tell me about things at Ch'ang-an;
For you entered just when my lute was tuned and lying balanced
  on my knees.'

GOING TO THE MOUNTAINS WITH
A LITTLE DANCING GIRL,
AGED FIFTEEN

(Written when the poet was about sixty-five)

Two top-knots not yet plaited into one.
Of thirty years—just beyond half.
You who are really a lady of silks and satins
Are now become my hill and stream companion!
At the spring fountains together we splash and play;
On the lovely trees together we climb and sport.

.   .   .   .

Her cheeks grow rosy, as she quickens her sleeve-dancing:
Her brows grow sad, as she slows her song's tune.
Don't go singing the Song of the Willow Branches,[1]
When there's no one here with a heart for you to break!

TO LIU YÜ-HSI

(A.D. 838)

In length of days and soundness of limb you and I are one;
Our eyes are not wholly blind, nor our ears quite deaf.
Deep drinking we lie together, fellows of a spring day;
Or gay-hearted boldly break into gatherings of young men.
When, seeking flowers, we borrowed his horse, the Governor[2]
      was vexed;
When, to play on the water, we stole his boat, the Duke of Chin[3]
      was sore.
I hear it said that in Lo-yang people are all shocked,
And call us by the name of 'Liu and Po, those two mad old men.'

[1] A plaintive love-song, to which Po Chü-i had himself written words.
[2] The Governor of Lo-yang.
[3] Po's friend and patron P'ei Tu, A.D. 765-837.

DREAMING OF YÜAN CHÊN

(A.D. 839)

AT night you came and took my hand and we wandered together in
    my dream;
When I woke in the morning there was no one to stop the tears
    that fell on my handkerchief.
At the Chang Inlet[1] your aged body three times passed through
    sickness;
At Hsien-yang[2] to the grasses on your grave eight autumns have
    come.
You—buried beneath the Springs, your bones mingled with clay;
I—lodging in the world of men, my hair white as snow.
A-wei and Han-lang[3] both followed in their turn;
Among the shadows of the Terrace of Night did you know them
    or not?

MY SERVANT WAKES ME

(A.D. 839)

MY servant wakes me: 'Master, it is broad day.
Rise from bed; I bring you bowl and comb.
Winter comes and the morning air is chill;
Today your Honour must not venture abroad.'
When I stay at home, no one comes to call;
What must I do with the long, idle hours?
Setting my chair where a faint sunshine falls
I have warmed wine and opened my poetry books.

SINCE I LAY ILL

(A.D. 840)

SINCE I lay ill, how long has passed?
Almost a hundred heavy-hanging days.
The maids have learnt to gather my medicine-herbs;
The dog no longer barks when the doctor comes.

---

[1] Near Tang-yang, central Hupeh.
[2] Near Ch'ang-an, the capital.
[3] Familiar names of Yüan Chên's son and son-in-law.

The jars in my cellar are plastered deep with mould;
My singers' mats are half crumbled to dust.
How can I bear, when the Earth renews her light,
To watch from a pillow the beauty of Spring unfold?

ON HEARING SOMEONE SING A
POEM BY YÜAN CHÊN

(Written long after Chên's death; *c.* A.D. 840)

No new poems his brush will trace;
    Even his fame is dead.
His old poems are deep in dust
    At the bottom of boxes and cupboards.
Once lately, when someone was singing,
    Suddenly I heard a verse—
Before I had time to catch the words
    A pain had stabbed my heart.

A DREAM OF MOUNTAINEERING

(Written when he was seventy)

AT night, in my dream, I stoutly climbed a mountain
Going out alone with my staff of holly-wood.
A thousand crags, a hundred hundred valleys—
In my dream-journey none were unexplored
And all the while my feet never grew tired
And my step was as strong as in my young days.
Can it be that when the mind travels backward
The body also returns to its old state?
And can it be, as between body and soul,
That the body may languish, while the soul is still strong?
Soul and body—both are vanities;
Dreaming and waking—both alike unreal.
In the day my feet are palsied and tottering;
In the night my steps go striding over the hills.
As day and night are divided in equal parts—
Between the two, I *get* as much as I *lose*.

ILLNESS

(Written *c*. A.D. 842, when he was paralysed)

DEAR friends, there is no cause for so much sympathy.
I shall certainly manage from time to time to take my walks abroad.
All that matters is an active mind, what is the use of feet?
By land one can ride in a carrying-chair; by water, be rowed in a
     boat.

THE PHILOSOPHERS

LAO TZŬ

'THOSE who speak know nothing;
Those who know are silent.'
Those words, I am told,
Were spoken by Lao-tzŭ.
If we are to believe that Lao-tzŭ
     Was himself one who knew,
How comes it that he wrote a book
     Of five thousand words?

CHUANG TZU, THE MONIST

CHUANG-TZU levels all things
And reduces them to the same Monad.
But I say that even in their sameness
Difference may be found.
Although in following the promptings of their nature
They display the same tendency,
Yet it seems to me that in some ways
A phoenix is superior to a reptile!

TAOISM AND BUDDHISM

(Written shortly before his death)

A TRAVELLER came from across the seas
Telling of strange sights.

'In a deep fold of the sea-hills
I saw a terrace and tower.
In the midst there stood a Fairy Temple
With one niche empty.
They all told me this was waiting
For Lo-t'ien to come.'

Traveller, I have studied the Empty Gate;[1]
I am no disciple of Fairies.
The story you have just told
Is nothing but an idle tale.
The hills of ocean shall never be
Lo-t'ien's home.
When I leave the earth it will be to go
To the Heaven of Bliss Fulfilled.[2]

LAST POEM

THEY have put my bed beside the unpainted screen;
They have shifted my stove in front of the blue curtain.
I listen to my grandchildren reading me a book;
I watch the servants heating up my soup.
With rapid pencil I answer the poems of friends,
I feel in my pockets and pull out medicine-money.
When this superintendence of trifling affairs is done,
I lie back on my pillows and sleep with my face to the South.

THE PITCHER

BY YÜAN CHÊN

(A.D. 779-831)

I DREAMT I climbed to a high, high plain;
And on the plain I found a deep well.

---

[1] Buddhism. The poem is quite frivolous, as is shown by his claim to Bodhisattva-hood.
[2] The 'Tushita' Heaven, where Bodhisattvas wait till it is time for them to appear on earth as Buddhas.

My throat was dry with climbing and I longed to drink,
And my eyes were eager to look into the cool shaft.
I walked round it, I looked right down;
I saw my image mirrored on the face of the pool.
An earthen pitcher was sinking into the black depths;
There was no rope to pull it to the well-head.
I was strangely troubled lest the pitcher should be lost,
And started wildly running to look for help.
From village to village I scoured that high plain;
The men were gone; fierce dogs snarled.
I came back and walked weeping round the well;
Faster and faster the blinding tears flowed—
Till my own sobbing suddenly woke me up;
My room was silent, no one in the house stirred.
The flame of my candle flickered with a green smoke;
The tears I had shed glittered in the candle-light.
A bell sounded; I knew it was the midnight-chime;
I sat up in bed and tried to arrange my thoughts:
The plain in my dream was the graveyard at Ch'ang-an,
Those hundred acres of untilled land.
The soil heavy and the mounds heaped high;
And the dead below them laid in deep troughs.
Deep are the troughs, yet sometimes dead men
Find their way to the world above the grave.
And to-night my love who died long ago
Came into my dream as the pitcher sunk in the well.
That was why the tears suddenly streamed from my eyes,
Streamed from my eyes and fell on the collar of my dress.

THE LADY AND THE MAGPIE

(Anon. Ninth Century A.D., written on the back of a Buddhist
scripture)

'LUCKY magpie, holy bird, what hateful lies you tell!
Prove, if you can, that ever once your coming brought good luck.
Once too often you have come, and this time I have caught you
And shut you up in a golden cage, and will not let you talk.'

'Lady, I came with kind intent and truly bring you joy;
Little did I think you would hold me fast and lock me in a golden
    cage.

If you really want that far-off man to come quickly home,
Set me free; I will bear him word, flying through the grey clouds.'

A PROTEST IN THE SIXTH YEAR OF CH'IEN FU (A.D. 879)

By Ts'ao Sung

(c. A.D. 830-910)

THE hills and rivers of the lowland country
    You have made your battle-ground.
How do you suppose the people who live there
    Will procure 'firewood and hay'?[1]
Do not let me hear you talking together
    About titles and promotions;
For a single general's reputation
    Is made out of ten thousand corpses.

IMMEASURABLE PAIN

By Li Hou-chu, last Emperor of the Southern T'ang Dynasty
(deposed in A.D. 975)

IMMEASURABLE pain!
My dreaming soul last night was king again.
As in past days
I wandered through the Palace of Delight,
And in my dream
Down grassy garden-ways
Glided my chariot, smoother than a summer stream;
There was moonlight,
The trees were blossoming,
And a faint wind softened the air of night,
For it was spring.

---

[1] The necessities of life.

THE CICADA

By Ou-yang Hsiu

(A.D. 1007-1072)

In the summer of the first year of Chia-yu (A.D. 1056), there was a great flood. By order of the Emperor I went to the Wine Spring Temple to pray for fine weather, when I heard a cicada singing. Upon which subject I wrote this poem:

HUSHED was the courtyard of the temple;
Solemn stood I, gazing
At the bright roofs and gables,
The glorious summits of that towering shrine.
Untroubled were my thoughts, intently prayed
My fasting soul, for every wandering sense
Was gathered to its home.
Unmoved I watched the motions of the world,
Saw deep into the nature of ten thousand things.
Suddenly the rain was over, no wind stirred
The morning-calm; round all the sky
Was cloudless blue, and the last thunder rolled.
Then we, to strew sweet-scented herbs upon the floor,
Drew near the coloured cloister, by whose side
Some old trees grew amid the grass
Of the deserted court. Here was a thing that cried
Upon a tree-top, sucking the shrill wind
To wail it back in a long whistling note—
That clasping in its arms
A tapering twig perpetually sighed,
Now shrill as flute, now soft as mandolin,
Sometimes a piercing cry
Choked at its very uttering, sometimes a cold tune
Dwindled to silence, then suddenly flowed again,
A single note, wandering in strange keys,
An air, yet fraught
With undertone of hidden harmony.
'What creature can this be?' 'Cicada is its name.'
'Are you not he, cicada,
Of whom I have heard told you can transform
Your body, magically moulding it
To new estate? Are you not he who, born
Upon the dung-heap, coveted the sky,
The clean and open air;

177

Found wings to mount the wind, yet skyward sailing
Upon a leafy tree-top checked your flight,
Pleased with its trim retreat? Are you not he
Who with the dew for drink, the wind for food,
Grows never old nor languid; who with looped locks
Frames womanish beauty;
Again your voice, cicada!
Not grave; not gay; part Lydian,
Part Dorian your tune that, suddenly begun,
Suddenly ceases.
Long since have I marvelled
How of ten thousand creatures there is not one
But has its tune; how, as each season takes its turn,
A hundred new birds sing, each weather wakes
A hundred insects from their sleep.
Now lisp the mango-birds
Like pretty children, prattling at their play.
As shuttle at the sounding loom
The tireless cricket creaks. Beautiful the flexions
Of tongue and trilling throat, how valiantly
They spend themselves to do it!
And even the croakers of the pond,
When they get rain to fill
Their miry, parching puddles, while they sip
New rivulets and browse the soppy earth,
Sing through the live-long night. And like enough
May frogs be passionate; but oh, what seeks
The silent worm in song?[1]
These and a thousand others, little and great,
Too many to name them all,
Myriads of creatures—each after its own shape and kin,
Hold at their season ceaseless tournament of song;
But swiftly, swiftly
Their days run out, time transmutes them, and there is
      silence,
Desert-silence where they sang.
                              Alas, philosophy has taught
That the transcending mind in its strange, level world
Sees not kinds, contraries, classes or degrees.

[1] All through the winter and spring the worm lives underground. On the first night of summer it issues and, in the thrill of its second birth, begins to sing in a shrill, woman's voice. It sings all night, and then is silent for ever.

And if of living things
Man once seemed best, what has he but a knack
Of facile speech, what but a plausible scheme
Of signs and ciphers that perpetuate
His thoughts and phrases? And on these expends
His brooding wits, consumes his vital breath—
One droning out the extremity of his woe,
Another to the wide world publishing
His nobleness of heart!
                    Thus, though he shares
The brief span of all creatures, yet his song
A hundred ages echoes after him.
But you, cicada,
What know you of this! Only for yourself
You make your music. . . .'
                    So was I pondering, comparing,
Setting difference by difference, gain by gain,
When suddenly the clouds came back and overhead
The storm blazed and crashed, spilling huge drops
Out of the rumbling sky. . . .
                    And silent now
Was the cicada's voice.

THE PEDLAR OF SPELLS

By Lu Yu

(A.D. 1125-1210)

AN old man selling charms in a cranny of the town wall;
He writes out spells to bless the silkworms and spells to protect
    the corn.
With the money he gets each day he only buys wine;
But he does not worry when his legs get wobbly, for he has a boy
    to lean on.

BOATING IN AUTUMN

By Lu Yu

AWAY and away I sail in my light boat;
My heart leaps with a great gust of joy.

Through the leafless branches I see the temple in the wood,
Over the dwindling stream the stone bridge towers.
Down the grassy lanes sheep and oxen pass;
In the misty village cranes and magpies cry.

———

Back in my home I drink a cup of wine
And need not fear the greed[1] of the evening wind.

THE HERD-BOY

By Lu Yu

In the southern village the boy who minds the ox
With his naked feet stands on the ox's back.
Through the hole in his coat the river wind blows;
Through his broken hat the mountain rain pours.
On the long dyke he seemed to be far away;
In the narrow lane suddenly we were face to face.

———

The boy is home and the ox is back in its stall;
And a dark smoke oozes through the thatched roof.

HOW I SAILED ON THE LAKE TILL I CAME TO THE EASTERN STREAM

By Lu Yu

Of Spring water—thirty or forty miles;
In the evening sunlight—three or four houses.
Youths and boys minding geese and ducks;
Women and girls tending mulberries and hemp.
The place—remote, their coats and scarves old;
The year—fruitful, their talk and laughter gay.
The old wanderer moors his flat boat
And staggers up the bank to pluck wistaria flowers.[2]

[1] Which 'eats' men.
[2] To make a rustic wine.

180

LOVE-POEM

By Fêng Mêng-lung

(c. 1590-1646)

Don't set sail!
The wind is rising and the weather none too good.
Far better come back to my house.
If there is anything you want, just tell me.
If you are cold, my body is warm.
Let us be happy together this one night.
Tomorrow the wind will have dropped;
Then you can go, and I shan't worry about you.

THE LITTLE CART

By Ch'ên Tzǔ-lung

(A.D. 1608-1647)

The little cart jolting and banging through the yellow haze of dusk;
The man pushing behind, the woman pulling in front.
They have left the city and do not know where to go.
'Green, green, those elm-tree leaves; *they* will cure my hunger,
If only we could find some quiet place and sup on them together.'

The wind has flattened the yellow mother-wort;
Above it in the distance they see the walls of a house.
'*There* surely must be people living who'll give you something to
    eat.'
They tap at the door, but no one comes; they look in, but the
    kitchen is empty.
They stand hesitating in the lonely road and their tears fall like rain.

Monkey   £1.95 ☐
The Way and Its Power   £1.95 ☐

*These books are available at your local bookshop or
newsagent, or can be ordered direct by post. Just tick
the titles you want and fill in the form below.*

Name..

Address ....

....

....

Write to Unwin Cash Sales, PO Box 11, Falmouth,
Cornwall TR10 9EN.

Please enclose remittance to the value of the cover
price plus:

UK: 45p for the first book plus 20p for the second
book, thereafter 14p for each additional book
ordered, to a maximum charge of £1.63.

BFPO and EIRE: 45p for the first book plus 20p for
the second book and 14p for the next 7 books and
thereafter 8p per book.

OVERSEAS: 75p for the first book plus 21p per
copy for each additional book.

Unwin Paperbacks reserve the right to show new
retail prices on covers, which may differ from those
previously advertised in the text or elsewhere.
Postage rates are also subject to revision.